Growing a Top-Notch Family Tree with Stories from its Branches

Nancy Blodgett Klein

Published by Nancy Blodgett Klein, 2024.

GROWING A TOP-NOTCH FAMILY TREE WITH STORIES FROM ITS BRANCHES

First edition. April 26, 2024.

ISBN: 979-8227066619

Written by Nancy Blodgett Klein.

Also by Nancy Blodgett Klein

Life Lessons: Guidance for All Ages
Torn Between Worlds
What's So Special About Spain?
Growing a Top-Notch Family Tree with Stories from its Branches
Poetry for Troubled Times

Watch for more at https://www.spainwriter.home.blog.

Table of Contents

For my mother, who first got me interested in genealogy many years ago.

Author's Note

To aid in finding the names of people discussed, I have boldfaced ancestors on first reference and included a list of all those relatives mentioned. People related by marriage are also boldfaced. People not related by blood or marriage, such as Alexander Graham Bell, are neither boldfaced nor indexed. At the same time, I thought readers might be interested in knowing what family names appear most frequently in my Ancestry tree, as some of these names may be shared by readers. I am listing here the family names that appear most frequently in my tree. Not all the families listed below are highlighted in this book.

At the same time, I want readers to be aware that genealogy is not an exact science. Despite my best efforts and search for reliable public records, not every person on my tree might be correctly listed by date of birth, marriage or death, and his or her connection to a relative might not be legitimate. If you see an error in my Ancestry, FamilySearch or Heritage trees, please send me an email from within one of these genealogy sites so it can be corrected.

Here are the family names that frequently appear on my public Ancestry tree Blodgetts and Delands Through the Ages. Is one of the branches of your family tree on this list?

Adams
Andrews
Atkinson
Beauchamp
Berkeley
Bethune
Birdsey
Blodgett
Bohun
Butler

Campbell
Capet
Church
Churchill
Clare
Clifford
Cook
Cooke
Cunningham
De Clare
Deland
Delano
De Lannoy
Douglas
Drummond
Dymoke
Ferrers
Fitzalan
Fitzwilliam
Forbes
Frank
Gordon
Grant
Grey
Habsburg
Herbert
Holmes
Hopkins
Howard
Johnson
Jones
Lamkin

Lathrop
Lothrop
MacCrimmon, McCrimmon
MacDonald, McDonald
MacGillvray, McGillvray
MacKay, McKay
MacKenzie, McKenzie
MacLean, McLean
MacLeod, McLeod
Maltby, Maltbie
MacPhee, McPhee
Mitchell, Mitchel
Montgomery
Morgan
Mortimer
Munro
Murrow
Neville
Northrup
Ogilvy
Oliver
Pantry
Percy
Plantagenet
Robinson
Roosevelt
Ross
Scudder
Seymour
Sinclair
Smith
Spencer

Stafford

Stewart, Stuart

Tudor

Warren

Welles, Wells

West

Wilcox, Wilcoxson

Wilson

Zealand

Countries, cities, or regions frequently appearing as part of last names in my family tree

Anjou

Aquitaine

Aragon

Bavaria

Bohemia

Bourgogne/Burgundy

Brabant

Castille & Leon

Flanders

Habsburg

Hungary

Kiev

Lorraine

Luxembourg

Normandy

Northumberland

Savoy

Saxony

Valois

Wormsgau

Introduction—Getting Hooked on Genealogy

"No self is of itself alone. It has a long chain of intellectual ancestors. The 'I' is chained to ancestry by many factors... This is not mere allegory, but an eternal memory." — Erwin Schrödinger, quantum physicist

Are you interested in genealogy and want to grow a top-notch family tree? Then this book is for you. It gives advice about how to be a good genealogist and includes stories from my tree-building experience to help illustrate the kinds of interesting information you can learn about your ancestors.

I've been a fan of genealogy for many years, especially since my mother and father passed away. Studying my ancestry was a way I could feel more connected to them and to their history. It's also a way to learn more about who we truly are because our genes and the genes of our relatives have a big influence in who we are and who we can become.

Genealogy also helps us better understand how we are all connected to one another. We are really one human family who share most of our DNA. It has been said humans are 99.9% alike in our genetic makeup. So we really are all distantly related if we go back far enough in time. Supposedly about one-fourth of Europeans are related to William the Conqueror.

If you are a fan of mysteries or whodunits, genealogy is a great hobby for you because you spend a lot of time uncovering mysteries about your family when researching genealogy. For instance, my great-grandmother seven generations ago was called Anna Ward. She died on May 19, 1771, and I found a wonderful write-up about her in a supplement to the Massachusetts Gazette published on July 11, 1771. Here is part of what the obituary said:

> She was the daughter of Mr. Obadiah Ward, a reputable family at Marlborough (Mass.). She was a person of superior natural powers, was very early in life truly virtuous...She was

applied to by her neighbors to keep a school, which she undertook and continued for 50 years and formed the children to the third generation to the knowledge of letters and good manners.

This is all well and good. She sounds like a relative to be proud of. But then read what the obituary said next. "She was a woman of sorrow and acquainted with domestic trouble beyond a parallel, all which she bore with patience and Christian fortitude." Oh really? What's this about, I wonder. This is an example of the kind of mysteries uncovered while practicing genealogy. It wasn't until I dug deeper into her family history that I was able to gain a partial answer to why Anna Ward was "acquainted with domestic trouble beyond a parallel." You will have to keep reading this book to find the answer to this mystery.

I have been building my public family tree since 2012. It has about seven thousand people on it and it's called Blodgetts and Delands Through the Ages. About once a week I go into my tree and refine it by discovering new relatives or make it smaller when I delete a person who turns out not to be related to me or not to have adequate public records to be included. I use the program Ancestry.com (referred to in this book as Ancestry) to build my tree. This program costs about forty-three dollars (USD) a month for access to records from around the world. You can also grow your own tree for free. The best free tree-building program I have found online is FamilySearch (familysearch.org).

Both of these programs are good and allow access to the knowledge and information of others working on trees that overlap with yours. One of the most interesting things I discovered when I first started to build my tree was how I was related to European royalty. Apparently, most immigrants who settled on the east coast of America in the 1600s had royal relatives.

If you can trace your family back to the time of the landing of the Mayflower (1620) or within a few decades after that, you will most likely find you are related to kings and queens. And because of so much intermarrying among royalty, once you find you are related to one king or queen, you will undoubtedly find many more royal relatives the further back you go.

At the same time, the further back you go, the more surprises await you. As I was growing the branches of my family tree of relatives once they had arrived in America, I found out I was related to many famous people. For example, I discovered while tracing my family line that I am a fifth cousin to Harriet Beecher Stowe, the famous author of Uncle Tom's Cabin. Even though I am six generations removed from being her cousin, the shared heritage is still there. Learning about family can also bring a sense of pride in who you are and the fine stock you came from.

How does one fall down the genealogy rabbit hole? For me, it happened when I discovered I was related to two passengers on the Mayflower. The two that I can verify via public records are **Stephen Hopkins** and his teenage son **Giles Hopkins**. Stephen Hopkins was a signer of the Mayflower Compact, a governing document for the first settlers in Plymouth Colony. Stephen Hopkins is my great-grandfather eleven generations back.

Hopkins first got shipwrecked in Bermuda for nine months on his way to Virginia before finally making it to Massachusetts on the Mayflower, according to the book Signers of the Mayflower Compact by Annie Haxtun. The write-up about Hopkins in this book said he had a "strong character." Sometimes this trait can be admirable but it can also lead to trouble. Because of the shipwreck, great-grandfather Hopkins said he didn't have to abide by the contract they had all signed since they never made it to Virginia. This assertion got him into trouble. He was court-martialed, convicted of treason, and sentenced to death. According to public records about this Mayflower passenger, "only the intervention of those whose favor he had won on previous good behavior saved him." He sounds like quite a character!

According to the General Society of Mayflower Descendants, there may be as many as thirty-five million living descendants of the Mayflower worldwide and ten million living descendants in the United States alone. Go to FamilySearch to discover if you, too, are related to anyone who came to America on the Mayflower. A page on their site asks the question: "Are You One of 35 Million Mayflower Descendants?" Then it prompts you to enter your ancestor's first and last name to find out. Here is the link: https://www.familysearch.org/en/collection/mayflower-descendants/

So if thirty-five million people have Mayflower ancestors, my having a genetic connection to Stephen Hopkins isn't that unique. Nonetheless, it sent me down the rabbit hole of wanting to learn more about all my ancestors.

The further back I went, the more I discovered about my roots. For example, I found out that **John the Fearless** was my great-grandfather twenty generations ago. He was a member of the French royal family who ruled the Burgundian State from 1404 until his death in 1419, according to public records.

Wikipedia notes that John the Fearless had a key role in French national affairs during the early fifteenth century, "particularly in the struggles to rule the country for the mentally ill King Charles VI, his cousin, and during the Hundred Years' War with England." It seems he wasn't a nice guy. He reportedly murdered the French king's brother, the Duke of Orléans, to gain control of the government. This, in turn, led to a civil war in part of France, which ended with his assassination in 1419. So Great-grandfather was a murderer and was murdered!

It was this kind of information about my ancestors that got me hooked on genealogy. Such discoveries about one's past can lead you to feel pride in accomplished relatives like Harriet Beecher Stowe, or pained by learning of relatives who were violent, such as John the Fearless.

Part One—-Growing a Top-Notch Famiy Tree

I think one of the most important parts of genealogy is growing a good tree. Much like gardening, trees require shaping and pruning to thrive. In the first part of this book I will be sharing practical ideas you can pursue to have the best family tree possible. Remember you aren't just building this for yourself. It's also for your children, grandchildren, other relatives, and the community at large. So make it special!

Indeed, part of my motivation for growing my tree and trying to make it exemplary is so that our two sons can access the Ancestry site and see who their ancestors were, on both my and my husband's side of the family, even after we are gone.

My husband is named **Richard Charles Klein** and I included several hundred relatives on his side in my family tree on Ancestry. He is German on his father's side and Norwegian on his mother's side. It remains like that for many generations with very little intermarriage among people from other countries. So it's interesting to see how different our trees are. On his side, there is no tracing back of ancestors to the Mayflower or any royal blood as far back as I have been able to go. Even so, gathering information about his family is an important task to do for descendants who want to know more about their family heritage. When some people pursue genealogy, they decide to grow more than one tree. For example, they would have a tree for their own family and then a separate one for their spouse. I originally decided to combine both my husband's family and my family onto one tree. But I have subsequently decided to have two separate trees, one for people interested in the Blodgett and Deland families and their ancestors, and one for the Klein and Munson family and their ancestors. With Ancestry, you can create more than one tree at no extra charge. At the same time, you can share your tree with others, as I have done with my fourth cousin **John Murrow**, a big fan of genealogy who I met while growing my tree on Ancestry.

Part Two—-Stories from Different Branches

The second part of my book will be a sharing of stories about my ancestors that will hopefully be of interest to you. Many of these relatives are people you probably already know something about, and in many cases these people might be related to you too. Some of these family stories illustrate the old saying that "The more things change, the more they remain the same." There is plenty of killing and suffering, as always, but there are also tales of accomplishments and good works. Let's get started.

Part One—How to Grow A Great Family Tree

There are many things that make a tree work well.

- *Verify your information.* Most important of all is that the facts you put in your tree must be as accurate as possible. Don't put in people you can't verify, or if you do, designate them as unverified.

- *Go back in time as far as possible.* An accurate tree with ten thousand people on it is a lot more valuable to other genealogists than one with one hundred people that goes back four generations.

- *Go deep.* Add as many interesting details as you can to people on your tree. Include web links to stories. Wikipedia is a great source for stories about famous relatives. Tree tags can help you go deep too.

- *Prune your tree.* You can do this by eliminating duplicate entries and deleting people who turn out to be unrelated to you.

- *Do a DNA test and use results to grow your tree.* These results can help you overcome brick walls and verify facts.

- *Decorate your tree.* A good tree includes photos, paintings, or other images of your relatives. As much as possible, try to get visuals for all your relatives. If you don't have photographs of them, at least put a flag of the country where your relative immigrated from on your tree or share a family crest if there is one.

Verify Facts

Remember not to trust family trees alone for information. Be careful when building your tree to not just mindlessly copy other people's family trees without any corroboration. If you find only two or three trees have certain information about your ancestor and you cannot verify this through other information, such as by checking birth certificates, death certificates, or census records, then don't add this person to your tree! Only add a person if you can verify his or her existence through public records.

If people are on your tree without public records to document their lives, I would suggest going into Ancestry and sorting the names of all your ancestors who are the End of the Line. These are the individuals most likely to lack documentation. Think of these people as the very tips of your tree branches. If a tip isn't well-defined, with lots of detail in terms of public records, I suggest trimming those tips off until you can find a person who does have public records to document their life. Often you only have to trim back one generation from the End of the Line to find such relatives.

If you are a task-completion type of person like me, be careful not to add suggested parents to a relative you have discovered without verifying whether they are indeed connected. It most commonly happens when your relative shared the same last name as someone famous and lived around the same time period and in the same part of the world as said famous person. For instance, I thought I was related to **Richard Warren**, a well-known Mayflower passenger, and linked up one of my female relatives to him. Then I discovered this was incorrect when I took more time to study their connections. Don't rush to connect people that don't belong together. Otherwise, you hurt the credibility of your tree. Plus, when you are wrong, you have to prune some branches that don't belong on your tree, and that's just making extra work for yourself.

You don't want to be the person whose tree others discount because it includes a child being born well after the mother died, for example. This is just sloppy ancestry work and you don't want to fall victim to it by copying this information to your tree. Other mistakes to avoid are giving a woman's date of birth as 1815, for instance, and then putting her marriage date as 1819. Be careful about such mistakes. Fortunately with Ancestry, the program will ask if you are sure about such dates. If you note that an ancestor was married in 1920, and had his first son in 1930, the program will ask you if you are certain about this date before you attempt to enter it.

Also, be careful growing a tree that gives four different dates for the marriage of a couple and includes them all. To me, this is like looking at a tree that has grown wild without anyone tending to it. It's unfortunate that you cannot give a date range for a marriage rather than having to pick a specific year in Ancestry.

You also need to be careful about photographs. Many times people will post a photograph on Ancestry claiming it to be one person when it is actually someone else. Don't just copy existing photographs of some relative to your tree unless you are pretty sure the photo is legitimately of him or her.

I noticed one person on Ancestry who posted photos of himself and his family visiting different historical sights relating to his famous relatives. No one wants to see that on Ancestry. He took selfies with paintings or statues of his different Pepin relatives like Pepin the Short and uploaded these as "hints" in Ancestry. No one wants to sort through hundreds of photos like that. Be respectful of other people's time when you add a photo or document to a family member on your tree.

The most important part of growing a family tree is verifying your facts, so I am devoting most of the first part of the book to how to do this.

Get Information from a Variety of Sources

The most important element of any family tree is for it to be accurate. In order to do this, information needs to be acquired from a variety of sources.

1. Use Reputable Genealogical Websites

One thing that can help you avoid tree mistakes and learn new information you might not find elsewhere is to go to different reputable genealogy sites. For example, the Church of Jesus Christ of Latter-Day Saints' site familysearch.org is an open tree where anyone who has an account can add information to the people on your tree. This approach to tree building gives you a much broader base of information from a wider variety of sources than you will have just growing your own tree on Ancestry.

When I first grew my tree back to the time of the Mayflower's arrival in the British colonies, I thought I was related to **Francis Cooke**. This was because a few people with their own family trees on Ancestry said that one **Josias Cooke** was the son of Francis Cooke. It wasn't until I looked at familysearch.org that I discovered that this particular Josias Cooke was not the son of Francis Cooke, despite what a few people had asserted. Public records have to support the people you are putting on your tree. You can't just make Francis Cooke the father of Josias Cooke because they share the same name and came to America from England during similar time periods.

On the FamilySearch site, I was able to verify that Mayflower passenger Stephen Hopkins was indeed my great-grandfather by linking my tree to information and public records other people had already shared on the site. That's why it's important to check reputable sites and not just rely on one site for all your tree-growing efforts. For example, I watched Uri Gonen, a SVP of Product at MyHeritage, discuss "Different Ways to Work with Your Family Tree." In his talk, he explained many features of this genealogical site, using his own family tree to illustrate what is possible to see and do. It was impressive and I learned about new features of the MyHeritage site I hadn't known about before even though I had been using the program for months. In fact, I was upset to find out I could have imported my FamilyTree site into MyHeritage once I signed up for the program rather than starting from scratch!

One really great feature of RootsTech is that when you are in the free FamilySearch site during the weekend of the conference (most recently held in early March 2023), you can find many relatives on different branches of your tree, and this can help you verify who belongs on your tree. For instance, on the Deland line of my family (my mother's side), I am related to **Jonas Abel Birdsey**, sometimes spelled Birdseye, who was born in 1750 in Stratford, Connecticut, and died in 1797 of yellow fever on his way to Cuba. When I signed into the RootsTech program that allows you to share your part of the FamilySearch tree, I found out that Jonas and his wife **Mary Northrup** had a son named **Abel Birdsey**, brother to **Phebe Birdsey**, my great-grandmother four generations back. Five generations down from Phebe and Abel was my fifth cousin one generation removed. Here is what this looks like:

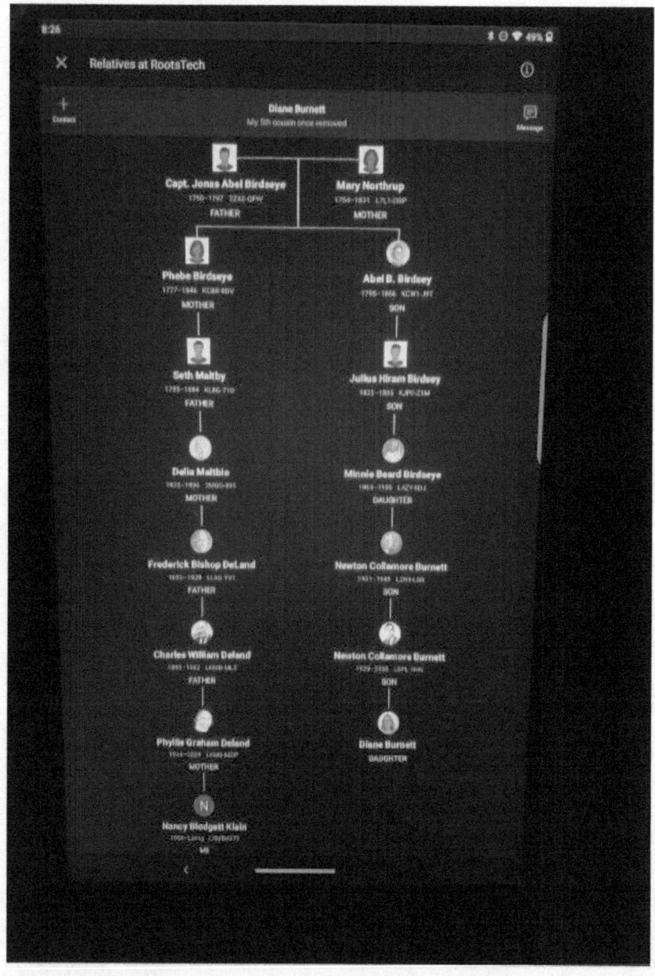

Seeing this information helps to verify who you have put in your tree. Getting information from several genealogical sites is also good because it allows you to find original material about your relatives that might not be encountered by sticking to one site. On the FamilySearch site, for example, I found a letter written about my great-grandfather that wasn't anywhere else. My great-grandfather, **Fred**

Deland, was my mother's grandfather. He was also a rambling man, having four different wives over the course of his lifetime.

Fortunately, Fred's first wife was a Mormon, and Mormons are big fans of genealogy. Fred had one son with his Mormon wife. After his son got married, he and his wife had ten children. One of his ten children wrote a letter to a coworker of Fred Deland's in Washington, DC, to find out more information about her grandfather. The coworker replied and Fred's granddaughter posted the letter about Fred Deland on FamilySearch, a Latter Day Saints (LDS) website.

I learned a lot more about my great-grandfather Fred through reading this letter. It is located in the Memories section of his page on FamilySearch. Fred Deland worked as an editor for a magazine published by the Volta Bureau, the headquarters of the American Association for the Promotion and Teaching of Speech to the Deaf. Alexander Graham Bell started this organization, and my great-grandfather Fred worked with Bell.

Josephine Timberlake, the executive secretary of the Volta Bureau at that time, wrote in the April 12, 1948, letter that Fred was close to his father but not to his mother, who, he said, "never had a good word for me."

Timberlake also wrote the following about Fred Deland, which is quoted in its entirety here.

I think the most important thing he told me about himself was about his education. He said one day that he had had very little opportunity to go to school, and I expressed surprise that he has been able to learn so much in spite of that fact. (He was very well read and had written several books and edited an electrical magazine, in addition to his work here.) He replied that he had acquired almost his whole education by himself, and after he was twenty years old. He said that when he was about eighteen or nineteen he was living in the West and got a job dragging chains for a group of surveyors. They were at a mountain camp one night, and three of the young engineers asked him to play cards with them. They sat and played, and he listened to the young fellows—all college graduates—talking to each other. "All of a sudden," he told me, "I realized that I didn't know what they were talking about. I didn't know what their words meant. I didn't know anything. It was the first time in my life that I had ever realized what an education could mean, and I lay awake that night and thought about it. I made up my mind that somehow I was going to be an educated man." He loved to read and study. If he got interested in any subject, he would read every word he could find about it anywhere.

Because of his great interest in telephone work, he became an authority on Alexander Graham Bell, the inventor, long before he ever met him. Dr. Bell said once in a letter, "Who is this fellow Deland? He seems to know more about me than I know myself—and the strange part is, he is right." Later he met Dr. Bell and became his devoted friend. Dr. Bell's daughter wrote him, after her father's death, that one of his last sentences was, "Tell Mr. Deland I loved him."

That is quite the letter, giving lots of details about what my great-grandfather was really like, and it's something I never would have found if I had just kept to Ancestry when doing my genealogy work. I can't stress enough the importance of going to multiple sources to get family information, visiting not just genealogy websites but also libraries.

Another reputable and popular genealogy site is MyHeritage.com, which I referenced earlier. For the purposes of drafting this book, I signed up for a one-year subscription to this site to see how it compares to Ancestry and FamilySearch. It cost about 150 dollars. It has some good features, such as sending notifications if new relatives have been found that are related to relatives already entered in your tree. This is called "Instant Discoveries." Rather than being one person, this is often a slew of people related to your ancestor, such as their father, mother, sister, brother, and children. So that's a nice bonus. If you accept the match, all these people are added to your tree. The downside to this is it often includes people you might not want to include in the grouping, such as the husband of the sister of your direct ancestor. But you have the option of whom among this group you want to include in your tree.

When I first started using MyHeritage, it felt like I was just making more work for myself by entering several generations of my tree into their site. However, I did find that the further back I went, I was able to obtain information about some relatives that I couldn't find on Ancestry or FamilySearch. For instance, when I was exploring my Scottish ancestors, I was able to find lots of information about relatives with the last name of Bethune on MyHeritage. And the information shared about these people seemed genuine as it came from relatives, albeit distant ones. Some valuable family information I found on this site about **Rev. John Ferquhard**

Bethune was shared by someone for whom the reverend was their great-great-grandfather's great-great-uncle! But in some cases, it's a direct descendent of the person who is sharing the information even though many generations removed.

Another bonus I discovered about using MyHeritage is the program will let you know when you have tree consistency issues. It actually has a Tree Consistency Checker that alerts you when you enter a child born after the death of a mother, a person that is too young or too old to have a child, facts about a person that occur before or after a person's birth or death, people married too young, spouses with a large age difference between them, or inconsistent spelling of a last name, among other issues. This is a great feature of this program and I don't believe Ancestry has anything similar yet.

Although MyHeritage has many good features, one concern I have with using it is that there is no way to merge duplicate entries, and these can crop up a lot in genealogy. With FamilySearch and Ancestry, you can merge duplicates: people with the same first and last name, same birth and death dates, and same parents, for example. But with MyHeritage you have to manually delete any duplicate entries, and this can mess up the tree you are working hard to grow.

1.   Go to Public and Private Libraries

I found useful information about the Blodgett and the Deland families, the birth surnames of my father and mother, at the Newberry Library in Chicago. The Newberry had a book about the Blodgett family that included my father's generation and went all the way back to Stowmarket, England, in 1604, from where the first Blodgett (then called Blowgatt) immigrated. This man was named **Thomas Blodgett** and he immigrated to the British colonies in 1635, bringing along his wife, Susanna, and his young sons Daniel and Samuel. He sailed on a ship called the *Increase* and landed in Massachusetts. Supposedly all Blodgetts living in the US today are descendants of this man. Thomas's younger son Samuel, who was two years old at the time of his immigration to America, is my great-grandfather ten generations back. Before leaving England, Thomas and his wife Susanna had several other children who had died in infancy. In an effort to save their remaining children from the 1623 plague that was spreading across Europe and England, they immigrated to the new settlement in America. If they hadn't done that, I would not be here!

When I was in Armagh, Northern Ireland, I went to the Cultural Heritage Service Library, where I used a computer to read news stories of the time some of my ancestors lived. I found a story about my great-grandfather three generations ago who had been robbed in Dublin. His name was **Richard Murrow**, a milliner with a hat store in Dublin, near the River Liffey. When he was living on 10 Haddington Road in Dublin in 1838, he was robbed. According to the *Drogheda Journal*, dated April 14, 1838, a servant girl named Mary Gordon stole items from his home and was caught by police a few days later. At this library, I had free access to Irish papers from the 1800s, which allowed me to find this interesting article about this particular Irish great-grandfather.

At this library I also learned about another of my Irish great-grandfathers four generations back. Francis Adams was robbed of his four guns, according to the May 9, 1797, Saunders's News-Letter. Other neighbors were also robbed of their guns, according to the news article. So if you want to include interesting information like this in your tree, make sure to visit public and private libraries that have genealogical information.

1. Read Family Histories

Genealogy books can be a big help in tree growing. But in addition to books in the library, you can also find good books shared online. For example, if you have Scottish ancestry and share the MacLeod name, I recommend the book History of the MacLeods with Genealogies of the Principal Families of the Name by Alexander MacKenzie. To find this, I had to Google Scottish ancestry and the name MacLeod, which led me to this book. It is free to download. To improve the quality of my tree, I read this book and others like it, keeping my tree open while I read so I could add pertinent information about my ancestors' history into the tree.

1. Check Out Find a Grave

Find a Grave (findagrave.com) is a great resource for photographs of deceased relatives to add to your tree. I have taken many photos from this site to add to my tree. Be careful about the biographies that are often included as part of the page with a relative's tombstone, however. Many times this information is inaccurate or incomplete. For example, only one child may be listed as part of the person's biography when you know for a fact that this person had half a dozen children. If there is no photo of your relative's gravesite but you know the cemetery where they are buried, you can request that a volunteer take a photo of this relative's tombstone for you. I had luck with this once. Unfortunately, many times your request for a photo of a relative's tombstone goes unfilled for years.

1. Visit Graveyards Yourself

Another way to try to find a grave is to go to a cemetery yourself in search of relatives. I have done this several times. I will share two stories: one visit was successful and the second time not so much. My mother's mother, **Naomi Graham**, had a sister named Ruth who died at twenty-one of pneumonia. She is buried with her father, **Samuel Ashmore Graham**, and her mother, **Rose Mary Adams**, in Oak Woods Cemetery on the South Side of Chicago. This was the area where they had lived before they died. However, the neighborhood where the graveyard is located has changed a lot since they lived there. I decided to go there anyway with my sister, her husband, and my fourth cousin John Murrow, who I had met and befriended through our subscriptions to Ancestry.

We went to the office and shared the names of our family members. They told us generally where the plots might be in the massive cemetery. After much searching, we finally found the gravestones of all three family members. It was a very meaningful experience and I am very glad we took the time to do that. Here is a photo of their plots, including the one for my great-grandaunt who died young. I also bought plastic flowers to honor my deceased relatives. That was a most successful trip.

While at Oak Woods Cemetery, I learned the Olympic runner Jesse Owens was buried there, as were civil rights activist Ida B. Wells and physicist Enrico Fermi.

Irish immigrant relatives buried at Oak Woods Cemetery in Chicago, Illinois

Tombstone of great-grandaunt Ruth Graham

Another cemetery trip wasn't so successful. A few years ago, I was lucky enough to travel to Florence, Italy, where I knew a relative was buried at a local cemetery. She was the aunt of Rosa Graham, whose memorial stone I have shared here. Her name was **Catherine Hope Adams**, my great-grandaunt only two generations ago. Apparently she never married and spent much of her adult life in Florence, Italy. I don't blame her. It's a beautiful city rich in history and culture. When I was there, I decided to walk out of the city to where she was buried in order to see if I could find her gravestone and take a photograph for Ancestry and also for Find a Grave. Catherine was born in 1835 in Monahan, Ireland. Her brother Francis, my great-grandfather, was a successful wool merchant who owned Monahan Mills in Ireland.

I thought I might have a good chance of finding her grave because I knew exactly when she died, February 15, 1909, and where she was buried, Il Cimitero Evangelico agli Allori (the Evangelical Cemetery at Allori). I walked there from Ponte Vecchio. It took me about forty-five minutes and I arrived while it was still open. I went to the office to get a map of the plots. But unfortunately, this cemetery only noted the plots for famous people, such as the Italian journalist Oriana Fallaci. Many other famous artists, painters, and writers are buried there, many of them from other countries. For example, the American Civil War general and artist Truman Seymour is buried there, as is John Wyndham Pope-Hennessy, a British art historian and former director of the British Museum.

I wasn't interested in seeing the famous people but instead decided to spend about one hour looking at plots in hopes of finding my great-grandaunt. Although I could clearly see the names of most people on the tombs and their birth and death dates, I wasn't able to find her. The cemetery was much too big. I didn't understand why they could not share information about the names of all the people buried there and show the general area where specific plots were located. But that was the way it was. I instead took a few photos of the cemetery, as it was pretty. Sometimes that's the way genealogy works. You get lucky once in a while and other times you strike out.

Evangelical Cemetery at Allori, in Florence, Italy

In addition to visiting graveyards, it's also worthwhile visiting museums where depictions of one's ancestors might be, especially if they were figures of historical note. For example, I was in Dijon, France, a few years ago, and visited the Musée des Beaux-Arts of Dijon. While there, I was able to see paintings of famous relatives as well as ornately decorated tombs that depicted what those ancestors looked like in real life. As noted earlier, John the Fearless is my great-grandfather nineteen generations back. In this museum, there is a breathtaking tomb for both John and his wife, **Margaret Wittelsbach** of Flanders, my great-grandmother nineteen generations ago. This is a photo of their tombs I took from above the Hall of Tombs.

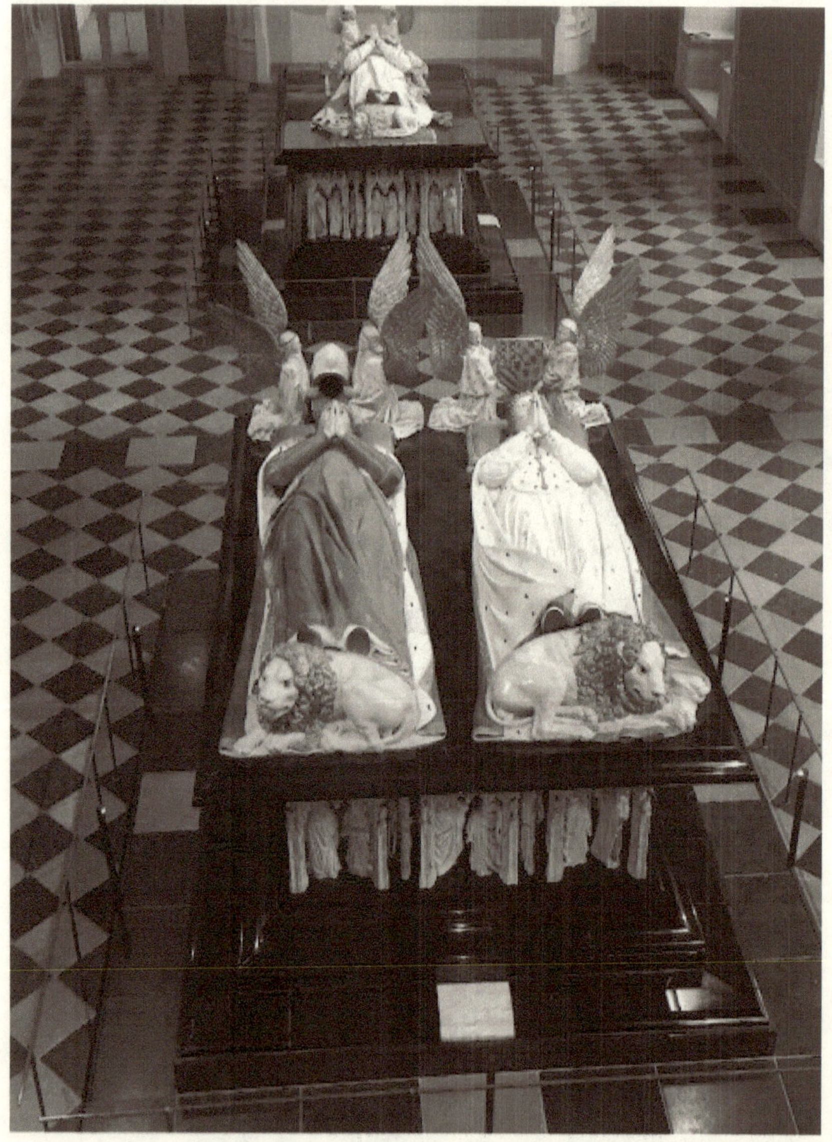

A close-up of the tomb of Margaret Wittelsbach of Flanders, taken from ground level

The father of John the Fearless, **Philip II of Burgundy**, has his own marble coffin on the far side of the room. It is also a very impressive work of art. He is known as Philip the Bold because he reportedly distinguished himself in battle while fighting in Poitiers, France.

Tomb of Philip the Bold, looked over by angels at his head and one lion by his feet

In this same museum, I was able to see and photograph paintings of other relatives connected to the House of Burgundy, including great-grandparents, such as Phillip II of Burgundy; great-granduncles like Philip the Good; and a first cousin, sixteen generations removed, **Isabella of Portugal**.

Wall of the Museum of Fine Arts in Dijon, France, covered with family relations

Isabella of Portugal. She liked to wear fancy head scarves.

Visits to museums to take photographs of ancestors is part of genealogy too. After taking these photos, I uploaded some of them to the appropriate persons' records on Ancestry. This way, other people could also use these photos if these individuals were their ancestors too.

1. Ask for Help on Ancestry, FamilySearch, etc.

Ancestry has a feature called Member Connect where you can see who else is researching your relatives and what information they have that you may not. Also you can contact people researching your ancestors by emailing them via Ancestry. I have communicated with many people this way, helping them gather information about relatives we have in common. You can also email other family tree builders on FamilySearch to get help, especially from those with relatives in common with you.

1. Join Genealogy Groups on Facebook

I did a search for genealogy groups on Facebook and found several possible groups anyone can join. *One is called Ancestry for All—Family History, Genealogy and DNA Chat, Tips and Help.* This group has more than thirteen thousand members. On this site, there are quite a few photographs family members have shared, where they are trying to identify what time period the photo might have been taken in based on how the subjects are dressed. For example, someone shared a family photo of their great-grandmother and wrote: *Can anyone tell me the approximate time period for this photo? We aren't sure if this is my great-grandmother, 1881–1986, or her mother, 1849–1910. We also can't agree on the approximate age of the person in the photo. Thanks so much.*

Another group member replied with the following helpful information: *She is wearing the high collar (Victorian style) dress. Like these ladies in a 1900s photo. This style was most popular in the 1890s to early 1900s. For her age she looks to me to be roughly 14–16 years old.*

The second Facebook site is called *Genealogy Family History Research Ancestry Tips and Tricks*. It has three thousand members. There are also people looking to identify time frames for photos of relatives here. On both of these sites, census records and death certificates are shared in the hopes that someone can correctly read what is written on these documents or interpret abbreviations or terminology used in the documents. Questions related to someone's DNA results are also common.

Of course, questions of a general nature are also asked on these sites. For instance, on the second site mentioned, someone asked the following question: *Hello! I'm looking to find out how to hire a genealogist (or someone who lives in Beirut, Lebanon) to help me get a copy of my father's birth certificate. I don't have much information on where to go or if any of it is online, so hoping folks have ideas of how to hire someone. Thank you!* Someone replied to her, letting her know there is a Lebanese Genealogy page on Facebook and sending her the link to it.

A third group I found on Facebook was called *Genealogy: For Beginners and Helpers*. It has more than four thousand members. A similar fourth group is called *Genealogy and DNA for Beginners*. It has more than eight thousand members. Undoubtedly, there are more sites than these four, but I wanted to give the reader an idea about what's out there in terms of possible resources.

You could even set up or join an existing Facebook group for people with your own family name. For example, I am a member of a Facebook group called *Adams Family History* as the Adams name pops up repeatedly on my mother's side of the family. Other people have joined Facebook family groups with successful results, including a member of my writing group, Torrevieja Writers' Circle, here in Spain.

8. Contact Living Relatives for Help

Since my tree is public on Ancestry, I get inquiries from time to time from relatives. Recently, a woman contacted me because her mother was my first cousin one generation removed. I gave the daughter, my second cousin, my email and she sent me her mom's phone number to contact. She was the daughter of my grandmother Norma Zealand's brother. After we had a nice long chat, we exchanged family photos with each other. I was so grateful for this because I had no photos of my grandmother Norma's sister Erna even though I had many photos of my grandmother and her two Zealand brothers, both of whom served in World War II. So it was great to have photos of the whole family. I really think it's important to get photos of family members going back at least two generations from my parents. That would be four photographs to cover all of my grandparents (going back one generation for each parent) and eight photographs for the previous generation, my great-grandparents.

Conversely, I can contact relatives on Ancestry or FamilySearch and get information or photos from them just by sending them an email. Most people are only too glad to help. I received pictures of my father's father from someone on Ancestry. This man figured out who my grandfather was based on my public tree and sent me some interesting photos of him. My grandfather is **Warren William Blodgett**. This is what my paternal grandfather looked like when I knew him. He was a lawyer and a conservative Republican, and I was a liberal Democrat, so we used to argue about politics at family dinners, much to the chagrin of my parents.

Warren William Blodgett, my grandfather

Grandfather Warren Blodgett in the US Army

My grandfather Warren Blodgett (third from left) with other soldiers from the Minnesota National Guard at Camp Llano Grande in Mercedes, Texas

I had never seen these photos of my grandfather as a young man, nor had my siblings. If I had not built a public tree on Ancestry, I never would have seen these pictures. This is a great example of the magic of practicing genealogy with others.

Apparently, my grandfather, who we called Bopa, was in Mercedes, Texas, in 1916, at Army Camp Llano Grande serving in the Minnesota National Guard. Camp Llano Grande was one of several US Army camps set up along the Rio Grande River in response to Mexican bandit raids into the US. The camp was closed in March 1917, one month before the US entered World War I. The troops that served there were then mobilized for service in France. Bopa was holding out on me. This was such an interesting part of his life and he never told me or any of my siblings about his experience as a young man serving in the National Guard by the Mexican border. Of course, he never talked to his grandchildren about his World War I experience either.

Based on my genealogical research, he didn't spend much time fighting in World War I. According to public records, Bopa served as a private in 126th B Field Artillery, Thirty-Fourth Infantry, in just the final two months of World War I. When I found out he actually did serve in the army during World War I, I did more digging into his life and discovered that he and his mates experienced a maritime disaster on their way over to France.

Bopa shipped out from New York City on the *HMS Kashmir* troopship on September 24, 1918, with hundreds of other men. After safely crossing the Atlantic and nearing the coast of Scotland on October 6, 1918, they encountered a severe storm. Another troopship, *HMS Otrano*, traveling in the wrong direction, collided with *HMS Kashmir* near the Isle of Inslay. Luckily, the *HMS Kashmir* made it into port at the Firth of Clyde, but the other ship didn't. The *Otrano* sank offshore, and although some men were rescued by another ship, 470 drowned. Most of the men were American soldiers or members of the crew. They never even got to fight in the war as their ship was destroyed by the heavy seas and the rocky coast. Hundreds of bodies washed up on the Scottish shoreline, piled up to 15 feet/4.6 meters high. How awful. Bopa never told us about this disaster, but it's a good example of the surprises you can uncover when doing genealogical research.

1.   Be Careful About Census Records

Census records can be a great source of information and can help verify where and when a relative lived. However, they can be unreliable or even comical because of the misspelling of names and the inconsistencies with dates. For example, my Irish grandfather Samuel Ashmore Graham must have told the census worker a different birth date every ten years when they came by to do the census, because his birth year kept changing. Where his parents were born also kept changing. First they were born in Scotland, then they were born in Ireland. He also claimed to be an orphan, so maybe he really didn't know when he was born or where his birth parents came from. But mistakes show up in many people's records, not just his. Misspelling of names seems to be the most common mistake I have seen.

So if the name on a record is spelled wrong but all information appears to be correct, I will typically include this record in my tree. I always get a picture in my mind of the worker at the door just writing out what a name sounds like without checking to see if it's correct or not. For instance, a German relative of mine named **Fred Bullinger** was written down as Fordin Bullinger in the 1870 US Census Records. My grandfather Fred Deland's name was written down in the 1900 Census as Fred Detanol with his wife listed as Rosa Detanol. Of course, surnames of all three children were also listed incorrectly as Detanol. Since the first names and ages of their children were all correct, as was the city of Chicago where they lived, I included this amusing record in my tree. You can actually report a spelling problem like this on Ancestry and they will correct it.

My great-uncle **Horatio Deland** was referred to as Horation Deland in the 1855 New York State Census. My great-grandfather **Seth Maltbie** was a postmaster in New York Mills, New York, in 1932. However, the public records of the US Appointments of US Postmasters 1832–1971 has his name listed as Set Maltbie, not Seth. So it isn't just census records that contain lots of mistakes. Other public records also make errors concerning the proper spelling of names and other information.

You really should be careful about any records you accept to your tree and make sure all facts are verified from multiple sources. For example, I was looking to find a verified connection to royal ancestors, and I thought I had one in Francis West, the Lt. Governor of Virginia. West is what is known as a gateway ancestor. If you can prove you are related to him, then you are also related to royalty. Most gateway ancestors lived in Massachusetts or Virginia in the 1600s around the time of the Mayflower landing and shortly thereafter. Certain people from that era are connected to royals in Britain, Scotland, Ireland, France, Spain, and several other European countries. Two books that list known gateway ancestors are *Ancestral Roots of Certain American Colonists Who Came to America Before 1700* by Frederick Lewis Weis, and *The Royal Descents of 900 Immigrants,* by Gary Boyd Roberts.

According to my tree records, my great-grandfather nine generations back was **Francis West**. I had linked him to Francis West, the Lt. Governor of Virginia, a confirmed gateway ancestor. Gateway Francis West was born in 1586 and died in 1634. He could well have been the father of my Francis West as they shared the same name and my ancestor was born around 1606 and died on January 1, 1692. So he was the right age to be the gateway ancestor's son. Geneanet

Community Tree Index even has the following hint on Ancestry as well.

Name Francis West, of Duxbury

Gender M (Male)

Birth Date 1606

Birth Place Probably, England, United Kingdom

Death Date 2 janv. 1692 (2 Jan 1692)

Death Place Duxbury, Plymouth County, Province of Massachusetts, Colonia, Massachusetts.

Father Francis West, Deputy Governor

Mother Jane Davy

Spouse Margery Margaret Reeves

Child Samuel West Sr; Abigail West; Francis West; Mary West; Peter West; Ruth West; Thomas D West

It indicates right there that his father is Francis West, the Deputy Governor.

Initially, that record was sufficient for me to link the two men together. Later on, however, I realized that the Francis West who lived in Duxbury, Massachusetts, was probably not connected to the famous gateway Virginia Lt. Gov. Francis West. Why would the father be living in Virginia and his son in Massachusetts? People didn't move around a lot at that time. I searched for more information to verify the connection between these two men and found out that other people had made this exact same mistake! These two men were not related. This is another cautionary tale to share so you don't link two people who aren't really related, despite what some public records or individual family trees might say.

Go Far Back

I would suggest going back at least ten generations to learn much more about ancestors from many years ago. This will also be helpful to others working on their own trees. Quite a few trees I have come across on different genealogical sites online contain only a dozen or two dozen people, with many of the people noted as private since they are still living. Although I give these people credit for making a start on building a family tree, such a limited amount of information isn't particularly helpful for others with more serious ambitions regarding growing a family tree. To go far back, checking other genealogy sites is key. FamilySearch has lots of good information for cross-checking with your Ancestry information. There are many other genealogy sites you can also check. Be aware that many of them cost money to access.

Here are some of the best-known sites besides Ancestry:

FamilySearch. This is the best-known, most reputable, free site.

MyHeritage. This costs money but it is good for helping you find and attach new records to your tree. When signing into the program, it will suggest matches for you to review from a variety of sources, such as FamilySearch, Geni World, Filae Family Trees, US Social Security records, and a number of census records from different countries and states. As a big bonus, it also includes some newspaper articles at no extra charge.

FindMyPast. This one is good for people researching British and Irish records. At the time of writing this book, they were offering a fourteen-day free trial.

IrishGenealogy. This is good for people researching Irish records. It works on a pay-as-you-go system so you don't have to sign up for a one-year subscription. This is not a definite list, of course. You may find another source that is quite helpful to you in tree-building. But, along with Ancestry, these are the four sites I have used myself to gather information to help in growing my tree.

Go Deep To Bring Your Tree to Life

It's important to grow your tree back as far as it can go as long as you have public records to support the information. However, to really bring your tree to life, it's equally important to go deep with the records you have of people on your tree. Don't just put the person's birth, death, and marriage dates. Find out what your relative did for a living, where they lived, what faith community they belonged to, if any, and what college or high school this person attended. If your relative was known in the community or famous, include links to relevant stories on their page.

Nowadays, many high school yearbook photos have been uploaded to Ancestry. These can be added to your tree, making a high school photo the profile picture for a relative.

Going to the library can be a big help in going deep. I was lucky enough to be able to visit the Public Record Office of Northern Ireland (PRONI) in Belfast when I attended a genealogy conference at Ulster Historical Foundation.

The day we went to the PRONI library, I found a copy of a deed in perpetuity of Milltown Mills signed by my great-grandfather only three generations back. His name was Francis Adams and he was a wool merchant. He was the same relative robbed of his guns I noted earlier. Born in Cornafean, County Cavan, Ireland, around 1800, his father was a lawyer and property owner. Both father and son attended Trinity College in Dublin. The dimensions of the legal document I discovered were huge. I estimate the parchment paper document to be three feet by three feet.

The envelope the three-page deed was enclosed in

Page 1 of the three-page lease in perpetuity on parchment paper written in ink with Francis Adams's signature and red wax seal

Apparently this lease agreement between my great-grandfather and one Henry Robert Lord Baron Rossmore was signed and sealed on August 16, 1852, in Dublin. The deed was entered into the registry office in Dublin on October 1, 1853. Baron Rossmore was named Henry Robert Westenra, third Baron Rossmore. He lived from 1792 to 1860 and was an Anglo-Irish Member of Parliament from 1843 to 1852. He was a politician and owner of many properties. Apparently, he spent most of his time in England so had no need for ongoing use of the Milltown Mills property.

Finding legal documents like this can be very exciting! At the same time, it can be very time-consuming to uncover such finds. In some ways, you feel like you are looking for a needle in a proverbial haystack. Genealogical work requires much patience.

Use Tree Tags

Besides adding photos and including other details, like photos of legal deeds from generations past, it's also a good idea to include "tree tags" to help you go deep. This can help your relatives and interested others quickly find out key things about the person they are researching. For example, I have a great-aunt named Grace Terry Deland who lived to be over one hundred years old, so I created a custom tag that said lived a long life. She never married or had children, so I also added existing tags for that. Here is a photo of how the tags look on her page in Ancestry.

Other custom tree tags I have added to my tree so far include, in alphabetical order: a murderer, accused of witchcraft, died after childbirth, drowned, executed, famous author, killed in battle, member of Parliament, murdered, namesake, politician, and religious figure.

One of my great-grandfathers I mentioned earlier, John the Fearless, was both a murderer and was murdered. So he has both tags on his profile page.

One of my grandmothers, **Norma Zealand**, was named after her father's sister Norma, who was killed in a train fire in Canada. Her profile includes the word *namesake* to explain that she was named after someone else.

Ancestry has created a wide variety of tree tags you can also use, such as *DNA Connections* (common DNA ancestor, for example), *Life Experience* (immigrant, for example), *Relationships* (multiple spouses, for example), and *Research Status Tags*. This last one includes such terms as *brick wall* when you can't find out anything about a relative's ancestors, and *hypothesis* as well as *unverified*. These last two are very handy when you aren't sure about someone's life facts and you want others to know that you aren't sure.

Add Supplemental Information

Another way to bring your tree to life is to include web links to your relatives. For famous people, I typically add Wikipedia or other online biographies so people can get more information about the person.

It's also good to include links to genealogical books shared publicly on Ancestry. For example, since my relative Stephen Hopkins is mentioned in the book *Signers of the Mayflower Compact*, I included a link to that book on his page on my tree. That way, people in search of more information about this person can look to the shared book for more details.

In Signers of the Mayflower Compact I found out great-grandfather Hopkins got into trouble not only in Bermuda but also when he came to Massachusetts. He got fined in 1637 for "permitting servants and others to sit in his house, drinking and playing shovelboard." He had little tolerance for the restrictions some of the Puritans imposed on the new settlers, and he came before the court on a variety of trivial charges over the years, such as for selling beer and doing it at too high a price in 1638, as well for selling a "looking glass" at too high a price in 1639. I included some of this information in my tree.

Working on my tree inspired me to learn more about this interesting ancestor. So I bought and read the book *Here Shall I Die Ashore, Stephen Hopkins: Bermuda Castaway, Jamestown Survivor and Mayflower Pilgrim* by Caleb Johnson. To provide you with a better sense of the captivating life and character of ancestor Stephen Hopkins, with Johnson's generous permission I include a paragraph from the epilogue of this well-researched book here.

The July 1644 death of Stephen Hopkins was a rather anticlimactic end indeed. Here was a man who has survived endless days of a hurricane onboard a sinking ship; was shipwrecked and marooned for nine months in Bermuda; lived for several years in Jamestown, witnessing everything from the greatest famine there to the marriage of Pocahontas; he had lived in Elizabethan and Jacobean England, walked on London Bridge, got his persona written into a Shakespeare play (The Tempest), and had invested in a bizarrely-organized joint-stock company founded by a bunch of religious Separatists that had fled to Holland. He sailed on the Mayflower, was attacked by Nauset, explored Cape Cod, and helped found and build Plymouth. He made missions to visit Massasoit, participated in the legendary Thanksgiving, lodged the famous Samoset and Squanto in his own house...and was a high-ranking member of the governor's council for many years.

I think you will agree that this great-grandfather of mine was a pretty impressive character, despite his legal troubles. I would love to have met him.

Finally, in order to grow a terrific tree, I make sure to save all the verified documents or photos of a relative other people have kindly shared on Ancestry to my tree as well. So here's an example of what going deep on Stephen Hopkins looks like on my tree.

This photo only captures half of the documents that appear on his gallery page in Ancestry.

Prune Your Tree to Keep It Vital

One thing you can do to keep your tree accurate is to eliminate duplicate entries. This can best be done on Ancestry by going into the search function from your tree and then selecting the list of all people. One way to review the list of possible duplicates is to look at your list of relatives, preferably in groups of one hundred if you have a big tree like mine, and then go through each page to see if you have any duplicate names with the same birth and death dates. If you do, then you should merge the two names into one person. If you have a tree with ten thousand names, for example, it will take a while to get through one hundred pages of names. Don't do it all in one sitting or you will lose your focus.

A less tedious way to eliminate duplicates is to just enter the last name of a possible duplicate. For example, I have a boatload of MacLeods because of my Scottish ancestry, so I enter the name MacLeod and all of them come up. From there, I can see the first and last name of all MacLeods. If the same first and last name appears twice or more, then I compare the birth and death dates and locations to see if any of them are the same. I then go into one entry, such as for Alexander MacLeod, and enter merge with duplicate. It's easy to make the mistake of having duplicate entries, especially with relatives with last names like MacLeod, which can also be spelled McLeod, MacCloud, or McCloud. Often times, Ancestry will already show one or more possible duplicates. By comparing facts, and if they are the same or almost the same, such as birth dates a few years apart but with matching death date and location, then they can be merged into one person. But don't merge the people until you also make sure both people also have the same father and mother. Doing this exercise many times can help clean up your tree and make it easier to follow.

If you really want to make your tree almost perfect and not only get rid of duplicates but also people you don't really want in your tree because they are too distantly related to you, you can put all the names in a list format and go through each person individually. This is very time-consuming but it makes a better tree. Go into each name and see if there are any public records for the person. If there are no public records, take the time to find at least one or delete the person. If you can find at least one public record and the person is closely related to you, even though they might be way back in time, such as fifteen generations back, then keep the person. Then make sure to include a picture on his or her profile, such as a flag from their country of birth. Going through a tree this way, you make decisions about who is worth keeping and who is not. For example, this may be the time to delete the paternal grandmother of the wife of your first cousin nineteen generations removed.

At a minimum, it's a good idea to see your tree in a list format and then filter the list by disconnected people. These are people in your tree who no longer have a biological connection to you. These might be relatives of people you deleted when you discovered they weren't really related to you after all. Make sure to get rid of these people or figure out why their connection to you is broken and replace the missing relative who should be there. Sometimes, when going through your alphabetical list this way, you may find people with little history. For instance, you might find Benjamin Stone and see that he only has a birth date, but no birth location, death date, or death location. When you see this, go into the detail and you may discover this is a distant relative, such as the brother-in-law of your great-grandmother twelve generations back. If you don't want to take the time to research this person, you might choose to delete him or her. Judgment calls have to be made. I will discuss this in more detail in the next section.

In any case, there are a variety of ways to filter your relatives in Ancestry that can be helpful. These include filtering by close family, direct ancestors, end of line, living relatives, and people with hints. For example, if you want to grow your tree, select people with hints and then go to the relatives with the most hints to go deeper with your tree building. Hints show up as green leaves in the top right-hand corner of each person's profile on Ancestry.

When asking that your family tree be shown in a list format, you might find that some of the names at the start of the list are not displayed alphabetically. When this happens, it might be because you put both the first and last name in the first name slot. Or it could be because you put a parenthesis around the beginning of a last name, such as one with multiple spellings of a last name, like Sir John (Bloteau, Bluitt, Bluit) Blott. Typing out a name this way will put this person before the beginning of an alphabetical list. So be careful not to begin the last name with a parenthesis in front of it.

Do you include all relatives of your relatives or not?

There is a debate in the genealogy world about whether you should include all the ancestors in your tree lines or just focus on the people you are directly related to, such as a great-grandfather, rather than a great-granduncle or -aunt, for instance. I think both approaches have benefits. Including a great-grandmother and all her siblings is more complete. But in many families in the past, this might mean including five to ten other siblings.

I am more of a proponent of going deep on the people I have, rather than making sure to include everyone. I don't include all my aunts and uncles in my tree, especially the further back I am going. The only lines in which I have tried to include many generations of aunts and uncles (but not all) are those from the Blodgett and Deland lines. I want to capture as many relatives of my father and mother going as far back as I possibly can without compromising the veracity of the information I am accepting or sharing with others.

Some people think you should include all the relatives of your great-grandmothers and great-grandfathers going back as far as you can. One advantage I can see to this is that if you get stuck at a certain relative, information about his or her siblings might help lead you to their parents. So that's always a plus.

The other instance where I will typically add siblings is when Ancestry lets me know I have some DNA matches, usually fourth or fifth cousins. When I see these, I will add the siblings of my close relative so that I can confirm that we all agree on who the great-grandfather or great-grandmother is. Thanks to advances in DNA testing, this is a scientific way to verify my tree.

At the same time, finding out more information about the siblings of a direct ancestor can also be very revealing. For example, remember back in the first chapter when I said genealogy helps you uncover mysteries? Well, by digging deeper into the siblings of **Phebe Green**, my great-grandmother six generations back, I was able to find out why her mother Anna Ward was "a woman of sorrow" with "domestic trouble beyond a parallel." Phebe had a younger brother named **Jabez Green**, born in 1710. According to The Worcester Book: A diary of noteworthy events in Worcester, Massachusetts from 1657 to 1883, shared on Ancestry, Jabez murdered Thomas McClure on September 29, 1741. According to public records of homicides from the time, Jabez "stab'd him in the Belly with a Knife, so that his Bowels came out, and he dy'd soon after." As a result of his confession, he was hanged on October 21, 1742. Jabez was Anna Ward's son and Phebe's little brother. Undoubtedly, having a murderer in the family was a terrible shock to everyone. It even upset me a little to have a great-granduncle like that. But it also explained some of the sorrow Anna Ward must have felt during her long life.

The other issue you need to make up your mind about regarding who is in your tree is whether to include spouses of relatives who are unrelated to you. For example, Richard Murrow, my third great-grandfather, owned a hat store in Dublin near the River Liffey. He was married to my third great-grandmother **Rosanna Adams**, the daughter of wool merchant Francis Adams. But she died in October of

1830, a few months after the birth of their fourth daughter. Later on, Richard remarried and had four more children with his new wife. So do I include this wife and these children or not? In some such cases, I would not include the second spouse or their children. However, when I am notified of a DNA match on Ancestry, I often find that the relative in question, often a fourth cousin, only shares one great-grandparent with me, not two. So if I want to verify that the relative I put on the tree has the correct information, including my grandparents' other spouse(s) will be helpful in this regard. DNA testing and matching is becoming a bigger and bigger issue in the genealogical world.

DNA Testing Can Help Overcome Obstacles

I highly recommend doing a DNA test to learn more about your own ancestry and also to help when encountering brick walls in your tree. When I paid for a DNA test from Ancestry several years ago, it cost one hundred dollars. I ordered a kit from the site and it was sent to me in the United States. I had to spit into a small plastic tube and then close it up and ship it off in a prepaid box. About six weeks later, I was notified that my results were available online. I share some of what I discovered here.

One of the many things I like about the results from Ancestry is they provide a pie chart that shows where your ancestors are from. That's how I found out I was more Scottish than any other ethnicity. Specifically, the results said my relatives came from the Ross and Cromarty area, the northwest part of Scotland. Here is my chart. Isn't that cool?

Ethnicity Estimate

● Scotland	51% >
● England & Northwestern Europe	34% >
● Ireland	12% >
● Germanic Europe	2% >
● Sweden & Denmark	1% >

Your DNA Story over time

Ethnicity   1700   1725   1750

Ancestry also provides information about the history of our ancestors over time. As you can see at the bottom of the photo above, it includes such information over twenty-five-decade intervals. So my family story tells about people leaving England, Scotland, and Ireland and moving to the east coast of the United States in great numbers. After many decades they started to move west across the US.

Starting with the year 1700, my tree includes a map of people moving from England, Scotland, Ireland, and Germany to the east coast of what is now the United States. It highlights two communities. One is where my family was coming from, the Scottish Highlands and Scottish Islands, including Ross and Cromarty. And one is where my family was going to, Connecticut and New York. It also includes a list of all the people in my tree who fit this profile. Isn't this great? Talk about bringing history to life.

The same places (Scottish Highlands and Islands as well as New York and Connecticut) appear in both 1725 and 1750 in my DNA story over time. But then in 1775, the story explains why more Scottish people were leaving. It mentions the Highland Clearances that took place between 1750 and 1860. This is when tenants were pushed off the lands they had lived on for many generations by landowners in order to make way for sheep farming, which was thought to be a more profitable venture.

Also, a new group of people appear on this part of my timelines. These are relatives settling in Southern Ontario in Canada. When the American Revolution ended, people who had supported the British, called Loyalists, left for Canada. The British government offered these people free land, up to two hundred acres. Scottish people from the Highlands also took advantage of this offer of free land to settle in an area called Upper Canada West. Lower Canada East was settled primarily by French Catholics.

Stories about one's ancestors' migration continue until 1925 on the Ancestry site. I think it's one of the biggest bonuses of an Ancestry subscription. None of the other popular genealogy sites like MyHeritage and FamilySearch appear to have anything like this. However, both of these other sites are also frequently updating their features, so this may change.

Comparing and Contrasting DNA Results

For the purposes of comparing and contrasting DNA test results for this book, I decided to take advantage of a special promotion offered by MyHeritage to get my DNA evaluated for thirty-nine euros. This company offered a special promotion while I was working on this book. The first difference in the two tests was that this one, done several years after the Ancestry test, had me putting long Q-tip-like sticks into the inside of my cheek. I had to do this on both sides of my mouth with two separate sticks. I then was instructed to snap off the bottom part of the sticks, put them in small plastic vials, and mail them to a place in Germany. The envelope they sent did not include prepaid postage. I was told by the postal worker in Spain that they would receive the sample within a week. So after one week I checked the MyHeritage site to track my DNA results, and a helpful "virtual assistant" named Eve said it might take up to three to four weeks to get my results after they had received them. I was also able to track that the sample had not yet been received by the lab. So I just kept checking. Finally, after about a month, I was informed that my sample had been received. Then I was emailed by Heritage at every stage of the testing process. Once the kit was at their lab in Germany, I was offered the chance to upgrade my results for sixty euros and get a genetic risk report that would "indicate my risk for developing conditions like heart disease, breast cancer, Parkinson's disease, and type 2 diabetes."

If I were younger, I might have taken advantage of this offer. But I am in my late sixties, so I know something like the conditions they listed may come for me sooner rather than later. Our bodies wear out. What can we do about it? Tree building is a constant reminder of our mortality as we enter a relative's birth and death dates whenever adding someone to our tree.

As part of the sixty-euro upgrade offer, MyHeritage said I could receive a carrier status report that "tells you if you're a carrier for conditions that can be passed on to your children, such as Tay-Sachs and cystic fibrosis." Too late for me as our children are full-grown and they fortunately don't have either of these conditions.

Once the lab had received my data, I received a report saying that DNA extraction was in process. It then explained what happened next.

21:23

MyHeritage DNA lab

Hi Nancy,

Your DNA sample is currently being analyzed in our CLIA-certified DNA lab.

Status: DNA extraction in progress

We wanted to take this opportunity to let you know how the sample gets processed in the lab.

Here is the process, step-by-step:

 Our technicians inspect your sample and make sure it's intact.

 The DNA is extracted from your cells in the vial and amplified. In other words, we make copies of the DNA in order to make sure we have enough of it to analyze.

 Your DNA is placed on a custom-made DNA genotyping chip and heated to a high temperature so the DNA can attach itself to the chip (hybridization).

 A computer reads the hybridized chips, producing the DNA data.

 Our algorithms process your DNA data and generate your Ethnicity Estimate and DNA Matches.

Best regards,
The MyHeritage team

MyHeritage did a very good job keeping me informed during the different steps of the DNA testing process. Not long after the extraction process was complete, I received an email from them saying my results were ready.

Once I got my results, I was eager to compare them to what Ancestry found. The way the two companies break down the results according to regions is different.

According to MyHeritage, I am 46.9% Irish, Scottish, and Welsh.

Ancestry isolates Scotland and says I am 51% Scottish.

MyHeritage says I am 28.5% English. Ancestry says I am 34% English and Northwestern European.

There isn't a way to make a direct comparison between these two tests. There is obviously an overlap in the findings. Both companies indicate I am mostly Scottish, Irish, and English. But then the results are quite different for the remaining regions. Ancestry's DNA test results show that I am 1% Swedish and Danish. MyHeritage, by contrast, says I am 8.95% Scandinavian.

Ancestry shows I am 2% "Germanic Europe." Apparently, Germanic Europe is Germany and parts of the countries nearby such as France, the Netherlands, Poland, Belgium, Switzerland, Austria, the Western Czech Republic, Denmark, Slovakia, Hungary, and Slovenia.

MyHeritage says I have 15.7% Balkan ancestry. That's quite a different result. There is no definite agreement on which countries constitute the Balkans. However, the following countries are often included in a definition of the Balkans: Albania, Bosnia and Herzegovina, Bulgaria, Croatia, Kosovo, Montenegro, North Macedonia, Romania, Serbia, and Slovenia.

The only country that overlaps Germanic Europe and the Balkans is Slovenia. So this is quite a mystery. Perhaps because I did the Heritage test in 2023 and the Ancestry test in 2016, a newer DNA test might pick up this Balkan connection. Or perhaps there are more people from the Balkans getting their DNA tested with MyHeritage than with Ancestry. In any case, when I reviewed the ancestors on my tree, I didn't notice many Balkan relatives. I did observe, though, that the MyHeritage map includes Hungary and part of Austria and the Czech Republic in its characterization of "the Balkans."

Thinking of this region according to the MyHeritage map, this makes more sense. I do have at least thirty relatives from Hungary on my tree. For example, **King Saint Stephen**, who established the country of Hungary, was my great-grandfather twenty-seven generations ago. He died August 15, 1038. His birthday is a day of national celebration in Hungary, with fireworks like one sees in the US on July 4.

In addition, **King Wenceslaus II of Bohemia**, who ruled from Prague, now part of the Czech Republic, is my great-grandfather twenty-three generations back. Born in 1271, he is considered by historians to be one of the most important Czech kings. He even had a song written about him called "Good King Wenceslaus" that people sing at Christmastime. Apparently, he had eleven children by two different wives plus many illegitimate children. So that might help explain my DNA connection to this region, after all.

Using DNA to Overcome Brick Walls

On certain family lines I have run into "brick walls" where I cannot find out any more information about a relative no matter how much I search on Ancestry, FamilySearch, or MyHeritage, or even just by Googling the person on the internet. I have found that by getting your DNA evaluated, brick walls can be knocked down in some cases because it is possible to find out about a relative who has DNA in common with you. That person can then help you build your family tree backward in time. Typically, the person will be a cousin of yours, and then you just start building backward from their tree to find the common grandparent. Most often the person with a genetic link is four or five generations back.

The DNA link can also help verify existing information that you have about your ancestors. For instance, when dealing with an ancestor with a very common last name this can prove especially helpful. I have a relative named **Thomas Cook**, born in 1781 in Ontario, Canada, and who died in 1870, in Ontario. There are thousands of Cooks in Canada. So the only way I was able to verify that this particular Cook was my great-grandfather three generations back was by seeing all the DNA matches I had for other fourth cousins of this same Cook family.

Following is what this looks like on Ancestry from my computer screen. I don't show photos of the three fourth cousins with DNA links to me here since they are all still living. However, this photo does capture two siblings, **William David Cook** and **Smith Cook**, both sons of Thomas Cook. The screenshot shows some of their descendants for three subsequent generations, including my father Charles W. Blodgett. He is in the second column down on the left. His great-grandfather, William David Cook, is one of Thomas Cook's sons shown here. On the far right tree branch it shows "private" at the bottom of the screen without a name or any birth or death dates. That means this person is probably still living, so they are not shown in the interest of privacy.

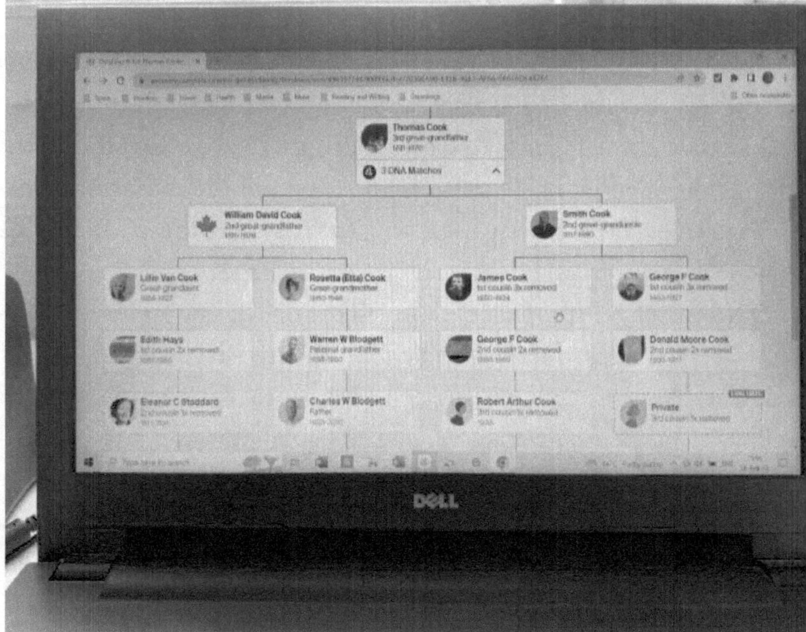

The feature of Ancestry that helps you find DNA matches for a relative is called Thrulines. According to Ancestry, "Thrulines shows you how you may be related to your DNA matches through the ancestors you share. You get Thrulines when ancestors from your tree are also in a match's tree."

Thrulines shows your parents and all your grandparents going back six generations. And if you don't have this all filled out going back five generations from your grandparents, Thrulines might suggest a person based on your DNA connection to someone else. I frequently go into Thrulines to see if there is any new or updated information on these five generations of ancestors. If there is a DNA match from a cousin sharing the same great-grandparent, for example, I will then add this person to the tree if he or she isn't there already.

Thrulines is a great feature of Ancestry. For example, on my mother's father's side of the family, I couldn't find out anything about a relative called **Eunice West Ingersoll**. I tried for years to get information about her and nothing worked. That is, nothing worked until I took another look at Thrulines and it suggested a new name for a grandparent I had never heard of. And what do you know? This checked out as I delved into the family history this cousin had posted on Ancestry.

Eunice West Ingersoll was my grandmother three generations back on my mother's side of the family. Born in 1803 in Albion, New York, records show that Eunice married **John Deland** on January 7, 1823, in New York City. John Deland is part of the Delano family tree, so any one of the thousands of people connected to this line might be interested in finding out more about this woman. I couldn't confirm Eunice's birth date, and this is probably a big reason I hit a brick wall about who her parents were. I was able to find a photograph of her tombstone, however, and this included her death date. So that was somewhat helpful.

Apparently there were lots of people named Ingersoll in New York during the time my great-grandmother would have been living. So when I looked at Thrulines recently and saw a grandfather suggested for Eunice, I was thrilled. Her father was supposedly a Massachusetts man named John Calvin Ingersoll, born in 1780. This information alone wouldn't have been enough for me to add them to my tree. However, because I had taken an Ancestry DNA test and so had a fourth cousin, I was able to see her tree and find the younger brother to Eunice. His name was Daniel West Ingersoll. These two people shared the same father but not the same mother. Through adding Daniel to my tree and then his descendants down until I connected with my DNA-matched fourth cousin, I was able to better verify the father of my grandmother Eunice.

As I built the tree further back on the Ingersoll line, I found the father of John Ingersoll. He was named Moses and his wife's name was Eunice West. So it looks like John Calvin Ingersoll had named his daughter after his mother, who died several years before his daughter's birth. This was another way for me to be more reassured I had the right information about my grandmother Eunice. Of course, I am still not 100 percent sure about this. One way to note uncertainty in your tree is to put the tag unverified on the person. That way, others can know that you aren't sure about this. Rather, this is just a hypothesis until you can prove it with sufficient DNA connections from other people with public trees.

When building your family tree, it's important to make sure the information you include is as accurate and verifiable as possible. If you have a lot of mistakes in your tree, other people will copy those mistakes and add them to their trees. Also, having a lot of mistakes means your tree isn't credible and that's not good either.

One of the sources of information I trust on Ancestry for information is called Millennium File. This site generally seems to have accurate information about people you might be researching. This is a much better source of information than copying someone else's family tree without independent verification.

In 2021, Ancestry bought a French genealogy company called Geneanet. This organization has a huge amount of records that can help verify what you think you know about a relative you are researching. Since they bought this company, I have been able to verify some facts I was struggling with about certain relatives. So I am pleased they made this purchase. Of course, they also make mistakes, too, as you will hear in another section of this book.

Using DNA Results to Help Others Overcome Brick Walls

I made friends with an English woman in my yoga class named Gillian Ann (Annie) Byles who told me her father was American but she didn't know who he was. Apparently, during World War II this man had been stationed at Grafton Underwood air base near Kettering, in England. One evening, he went to a dance where he met my yoga friend's mother. One thing led to another and she became pregnant with my friend Annie. He may never have known about her existence. All she knew about her father was he had been an American navigator at an air base in England near where her mother lived and he had the nickname "Choggy." For many months, I tried to help her find out who her dad was but couldn't make progress without a specific name and date of birth.

Annie came to yoga one day and told me she now had her DNA results from Ancestry that showed she had a 50 percent match with a woman in the United States, most likely a half-sister. I asked her to give me that person's name and where she lived. With this information, I was able to find out who Annie's father was in the Army Air Force!

At our next yoga class, I showed her his handsome photograph on Ancestry, gave her his name, his birth date, and, sadly, his death date. Annie was never able to meet up with him. However, she does have a half-sister and two half-brothers in Texas who she has since been in contact with over the course of the past several years. In fact, one of her half-brothers, Tom, even visited Annie in Spain.

We discovered that her father's name was William Page Buckle Jr. He was born February 6, 1911, in Ohio. He died January 30, 1982, in Houston, Texas. Annie's father went overseas in June of 1942 and was a member of the Ninety-Seventh Bombardment Group of the Army Air Force. During his service in World War II, he earned the Distinguished Flying Cross and the Air Medal with nine Oak Leaf Clusters. He had seventeen months of combat duty and flew fifty-two missions in a B-57 Flying Fortress plane. Captain Buckle even participated in the first American bombing raid over Rouen, France. He was quite the hero. I found his photograph on Ancestry and brought it to yoga class to show my friend Annie. "This is your father," I told her.

William Page Buckle Jr., father of my English friend and yoga classmate

Annie was thrilled to see the photo and learn that her father had been a hero during WWII. She also told a local newspaper when interviewed about this discovery that, "I'm just pleased to now know who my father was. I don't feel sad about the missing years. I just feel proud Dad did his duty for our freedom today."

Later on, Annie shared a photo with me of her father and her grandson. The resemblance between these two men is uncanny, especially the shape of the ears and the style of the nose. In this case having DNA results and using Ancestry helped me to help Annie find out who her father was. She was very grateful for my assistance. But I couldn't have done it if Annie had not done a DNA test herself and shared her results on Ancestry. It was lucky her half-sister in Texas decided to do the same thing.

Brick Walls That Remain

Sometimes you won't be able to overcome brick walls no matter what you do. My great-grandfather Samuel Ashmore Graham was born in Larne, County Antrim, Northern Ireland in either 1842 or 1844.

Larne is one of two port cities in County Antrim, the other being Belfast. I have two different dates for his birth and I am not sure either one is correct. According to my mother, Sam Graham claimed he was an orphan. We don't have any details about what happened to his birth parents.

When I was in Ireland in 2017, I tried to find out more information about this relative. But since his actual birth date wasn't known, I thought that perhaps I could find out more about who his parents might be or gather information about his older brothers and sisters if he had any. When I went to the Public Records Office of Northern Ireland (PRONI), which is right next to the Titanic Museum by the way, I thought I would be able to solve some mysteries about him there. Since my great-grandfather was born in the early 1840s, I was hoping to take a look at the Irish Census records from 1821, 1831, and 1841 to perhaps turn up information about his father, who might have also lived in the Larne or Belfast area and could have been named Samuel Ashmore Graham as well.

I learned that the Irish Censuses of 1821, 1831, 1841, and 1851 were burned in the Public Records Office located in the Four Courts government building. These and other records were lost during the Irish Civil War on June 30, 1922, when an explosion and fire destroyed much of the Four Courts government building after two days of government bombardment. Members of the Irish Republican Army had occupied the building since mid-April of the same year. The civil war was fought between the Provisional Government of Ireland and the IRA over the Anglo-Irish Treaty. It was members of the IRA's Anti-Treaty group that occupied the Four Courts building.

For now, I only have information about Samuel Ashmore Graham from when he immigrated to the United States. According to US Census records, he was naturalized as a US citizen in 1875, when he would have been between twenty-one and twenty-three years old. So he must have come over to the United States when he was quite young. I hope that someday I will find out more information about this relative, whose branch of my tree ends abruptly with him.

Decorate Your Tree with Relevant Images

To grow a great family tree, it is important to include as many relevant images as possible of your relatives. Get photos from family for recently deceased family members. Verify that the photos you already have of family include the names of people on the back. When my mother-in-law died, we were given dozens of photos of family. However, we didn't know who most of the people were because she hadn't written their names or dates on most of the photos. In some cases, we were able to identify some people because my husband's aunt (who is now in her nineties) helped us with some of the photos that had been taken during her lifetime. But in most cases, we weren't able to use the ancestor photos because we didn't know who the people were and didn't want to put any inaccurate information on the tree by guessing.

If any of your ancestors are famous, such as my cousins Franklin Delano Roosevelt or Ulysses S. Grant, you won't have any trouble including photos in your tree. You will probably have too many to choose from. If you have famous relatives from the time before photography, you might have paintings of these people, especially if they were royals or of high social rank. Include these paintings in your tree. But, again, make sure the painting is of the person you think it is, rather than just thoughtlessly copying something from someone else's tree who says this is person X. If you don't have photos or paintings, you can include a family castle if your ancestors lived in one. Or, if that's not possible, you can always include a flag of the country where your ancestor is from. My tree is filled with flags of Scotland and Germany. Flags of regions are also good. I have quite a few ancestors with flags from the Devon region of England. Another option I recommend is to include a family crest for the person, especially if no photos or paintings are available and you want to have some variety in your family tree, rather than always using flags as the default option.

If you can't find a photo, painting, or family crest and you are tired of using a flag to signify a country or region where your ancestor was born, you can opt for including a photo of a part of the city or town where the person was from or even a photo of a map of the relative's birthplace. That will give your tree branches more variety. You can even use a photo of a person's tombstone if nothing else works. I try to find some visual of interest for every ancestor on my tree, if possible.

Part Two—Family Stories from Tree Branches

Learning about one's relatives can be a source of shame or pride based on how these people lived their lives. As I mentioned earlier, I discovered that Harriet Beecher Stowe, author of Uncle Tom's Cabin, is my fifth cousin six generations removed. But I also learned **Henry David Thoreau** is my sixth cousin five generations removed. He is the famous author of *Walden* and other well-known works.

US President **Ulysses Grant** is my fifth cousin five generations removed while US President **Franklin Delano Roosevelt** was my sixth cousin four generations removed. Learning this filled me with pride. But it also made me wonder where I got my drive to write. Might some of their genealogical programming have been passed on to me?

Grant was an author and finished his personal memoirs shortly before he died. President Roosevelt published many books. When I feel a compulsion to write a blog post, a magazine article, or a book, I wonder if that is partly because the blood of other authors runs through my veins. One wonders whether shared DNA can also mean shared destiny?

Of course, being related to these impressive people isn't much of an accomplishment by itself. It's more luck of the draw, not something I did but something I inherited upon my birth because of the ancestry of my mother's father, **Charles William Deland**. His surname used to be Delano or Delane but was changed to Deland after several generations of ancestors lived in America. Party because of the Delano connection, Grant and FDR are related to each other and to me. Harriet Beecher Stowe hooked into the Deland line more recently, about the same time period as she was living.

What I admire about these ancestors isn't just that they were published authors and well-known public figures but that they were honorable characters. Who they were as people attracts me to them. What were the positive traits that stand out among these four ancestors?

Harriet Beecher Stowe was born June 14, 1811. One of the character traits she was known for was her integrity. She opposed slavery and used her intellect to write and publish a book opposing this unjust practice, at a time when many other white people were fine with it. She was brave, and not afraid to speak truth to power. This was all the more remarkable because when she published the anti-slavery book *Uncle Tom's Cabin* in 1851, women authors were not common. This made her doubly brave, to both highlight the cruelty of slavery when many Southerners, in particular, supported the practice and to speak out publicly as a woman author. The publication of her book helped open the eyes of more white people, turning many against the institution of slavery.

Henry David Thoreau was born July 12, 1817. He was an individualist, unafraid to confront others on behalf of his principles. He refused to pay a poll tax and spent a night in jail as a result. He used this time in jail to write a now famous essay on civil disobedience. This essay argues for disobedience to law when the state is unjust in its actions, such as when it allows the cruel and unjust practice of slavery. To write and publish such an essay took a lot of courage, just as Beecher Stowe showed courage for publishing her book when she did. They were both ardent abolitionists.

Thoreau is famous for his book *Walden*, where he decided to live simply and alone out in the woods. Why did he do this? He explained in *Walden*:

> I went to the woods because I wished to live deliberately, to front only the essential facts of life, and see if I could not learn what it had to teach, and not, when I came to die, discover that I had not lived. I did not wish to live what

was not life, living is so dear; nor did I wish to practice resignation, unless it was quite necessary. I wanted to live deep and suck out all the marrow of life, to live so sturdily and Spartan-like as to put to rout all that was not life, to cut a broad swath and shave close, to drive life into a corner, and reduce it to its lowest terms...

This part of Thoreau's book made such a great impression on me when I read it in high school that I decided to major in philosophy in college. This would allow me to read more books of wisdom and depth, more books that were searching for life's meaning. Ulysses S. Grant was born April 27, 1822. As General Grant, he showed great courage in leading the Union army in many battles to end the Civil War and keep the country united. He was a humble man who didn't put on airs and treated everyone with respect. Grant was also an honest man, although when he was president others around him were not as honest. His trust in others hurt him both politically and financially.

As president, Grant worked hard to bring about reconciliation between the North and the South after the Civil War was over. The Fifteenth Amendment was passed under the Grant administration, giving Black men the right to vote. Grant also tried to limit activities of groups like the Ku Klux Klan that used violence to intimidate Black people and prevent them from voting.

Franklin Delano Roosevelt (FDR) was born January 30, 1882. He was a man of principle and action. He was famous for saying, "We have nothing to fear but fear itself." Roosevelt had the leadership skills to guide the US through the Great Depression and most of World War II. He also recognized that without help from the US, Britain might lose WWII, and Hitler would then control all of Europe. So FDR did what he could to help British Prime Minister Winston Churchill and the United Kingdom until he could bring the American public on board to directly support the Allies in the war. And he did all this while suffering from the aftereffects of polio!

So what do these four ancestors have in common? They were all people of integrity and principle. They were courageous and willing to take a stand even at their own expense. They understood that every person has worth and dignity, not just some people. Another writer I am related to that isn't connected to the Deland family line is **Ralph Waldo Emerson**. He is my fifth cousin, like Harriet Beecher Stowe, but only five generations removed. Like Harriet Beecher Stowe, he was also an ardent abolitionist. He was a man of many talents: an essayist, lecturer, philosopher, and poet who led the transcendentalist movement in the mid-1800s. He was also friends with Henry David Thoreau.

As you can see from this story about my relatives, when you are studying your roots, you are also studying history. While some of the history you learn may fill you with pride, other information you uncover about your family history will likely bring you pain. Here is an example of one such tale.

Six Generations of Sad Endings

While growing my family tree on my father's mother's side, I discovered it is filled with pain and loss for one hundred years straight. One line in particular had six generations in a row of family catastrophes. Men in this family just kept dying in all kinds of tragic ways. This is the Zealand line.

Death at an early age is not uncommon in most families, especially for people living during or before the early 1900s. In fact, both my mother's mother and my mother's father had sisters who died young. One of my mother's aunts died in 1909 of pneumonia at the age of twenty-one, while my mother's other aunt died in 1921 of influenza at the age of thirty, leaving behind a husband and two daughters.

Of course, death by pneumonia, influenza, or other contagious illnesses like tuberculosis was commonplace in the early part of the twentieth century. But it is the way in which the Zealand men died that caught my attention as it was always so sudden, so tragic, and so constant through six generations.

Let's begin with **Edward William Zealand Sr**. He is my grandfather three generations back. He was born in 1793 in Scarborough, in Yorkshire, England. By the time he was twenty, he had immigrated to Ontario, Canada, and was serving in the British Navy there. Perhaps this was how he got experience to become a sea captain himself. In time, Captain Edward Zealand married and had six sons with his wife. By 1840, he had his own wharf and transport business.

Seven years later, Zealand had three schooners as part of his business. Thankfully, this successful Ontario resident lived a long life. But death came for him suddenly in 1869 when he was gored by a cow that had escaped from the market. According to a book about Hamilton Canada residents, "this well-known sea captain was buried in the Hamilton, Ontario, cemetery with "full military honors."

Most of Edward Zealand's sons also became sailors. His oldest son, **Edward Gordon Zealand Jr.**, was born in 1829. Though not my grandfather, this son drowned on the ship *Zealand* that went down in a storm in Lake Ontario in November 1880. He was fifty-one years old. At least eight other people died with him.

Officers and Crew of the Zealand.

[Associated Press Dispatch.]

TORONTO, November 11.—The following is the most complete list that can be obtained of the names of the officers and crew of the propeller Zealand, believed to be lost in the gale of Saturday night: Edward Zealand, captain, Hamilton; Thomas Dewey, first engineer, St. Catharines; David Taylor, second engineer, Port Colborne; Joseph Malette, first mate, Montreal; Thos. Daros Ligic, second mate, Cornwall; Thos. Armstrong, carpenter, Hamilton; Miss Frances, lady's maid, Montreal; two deck hands who were known on board as George and Jack, the fromer from England, and the latter belonging to Toronto. Capt. Thos. Zealand, brother of the deceased, and his son have left for the north shore to search for the wreck or bodies.

The Captain of the Missing Zealand.

Capt. Edward Zealand is well and favorably known to all sailors on Lake Ontario. He was born and bred a sailor. His father was the well-known Capt. Edward Zealand, who was the last man on board the notorious steamer Caroline, which was sent over Niagara Falls in 1812. The late Capt. Zealand has been a lake captain all his life, and has commanded some of the best vessels on the lower lakes. He was a citizen of Hamilton, where he leaves a wife and a large family. His sailor's life has been full of adventures. He has been wrecked several times, and escaped all dangers, to go down unseen in one of the worst storms that ever swept Ontario.

One of the younger brothers of Edward Gordon Zealand Jr. was my grandfather two generations back. Unlike his brothers, he was not a sailor. But he died a horrible death anyway. **Samuel Gordon Zealand** was born in 1840 in Hamilton, Ontario, where he lived a more ordinary life. He married in 1866 and had three children. His first wife died, and two years later, in 1874, Sam Zealand married again. With his new wife, **Sarah Holmes**, a lady of English descent, he had two sons and a daughter. One of his sons, Charles Herbert (Bert) Zealand, is my great-grandfather.

On July 15, 1887, Samuel, wife Sarah, and baby Norma all took a ride on a train to go to a church picnic. On the way back, the passenger train ran into a freight train loaded with oil, which set fire to both trains, including in the cabin where my relatives sat. All three of them died from burns. This event was known as the St. Thomas Train Disaster and it was a big news event, as you might imagine. According to news stories at the time, at least twenty-five people died then or shortly thereafter from burns.

According to news reports of the tragedy, my great-grandfather Sam Zealand, a clerk at Nickleborough's Dry Goods Store, died from burns sustained in the blaze along with his one-year-old daughter, Norma. His wife was badly burned and died shortly afterwards. My great-grandfather Bert was either in a different part of the train or didn't attend the picnic. He was nine years old at the time of this catastrophe.

Great-grandfather Bert ultimately recovered from this terrible tragedy, married a woman named Christina (Tena) McKay, who was of Scottish descent, and had four children. His older brother, Theo, who was twelve at the time of the train wreck, never married or had children.

They had four children, including my grandmother Norma, named after Bert's sister who died in the train wreck. Bert and Tena had three other children: a daughter named Erma, and two sons. All was well until World War II started in 1939. Then both sons went off to fight in the war. One son, Gordon, came back home alive. Their other son, my great-uncle, was killed after the heroic taking of Remagen Bridge in Germany on March 7, 1945. The capture of this key bridge over the Rhine River enabled the allies to move east more quickly and helped end the war sooner. https://en.wikipedia.org/wiki/Ludendorff_Bridge.

My great-uncle's name was **Donald Edward Zealand**. He was a Lieutenant Colonel in the army, and he must have done some impressive things during his war service because I have a photo of him receiving a Bronze Star medal for "meritorious achievement in connection with operations against the enemy."

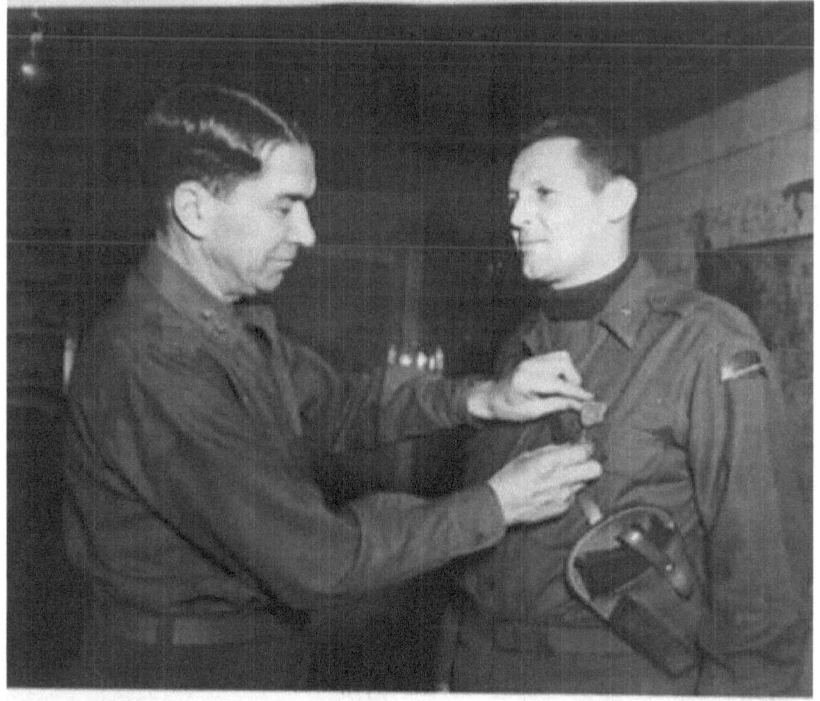

Major General Edwin Parker, Commanding General Seventy-Eighth Lightning Division, presenting Lt. Col. Donald E. Zealand with

Bronze Star Medal for "meritorious achievement in connection with operations against the enemy"

My great-uncle Donald Zealand was buried in Liege, Belgium, at Henri-Chapelle American Cemetery and Memorial. My great-grandfather Bert didn't die suddenly like some of my other male Zealand relatives, but he was certainly touched by tragedy with the sudden death of his parents, baby sister, and later the death of one of his sons.

I have covered four generations of Zealands so far, but now we get to
the really hard stuff that personally affected me as I lived through it.
Donald Zealand was the brother of my grandmother Norma. I didn't
realize until I started getting deeply interested in genealogy that she

was named after the baby who died in the St. Thomas Train Disaster. Little kids are often protected from these sad stories, and by the time we want to know about such things, the people to ask have already died.

My grandmother Norma had two children with her husband Warren Blodgett: **Virginia Blodgett** and my father, **Charles Warren Blodgett**. My aunt Virginia had a successful career as a clothes designer in New York City. She had bad luck with men, however, and married a Dutch sailor who wasn't nice to her. After having a son together called Donald Edward, named after his deceased uncle Donald Edward Zealand, they split up. Her husband was later deported to Holland. Her life then revolved around her son, my cousin Donald. All was well until the Vietnam War, when cousin Donald decided to become a navy medic. He could have stayed stateside but chose not to.

Donald died on April 1, 1968, after suffering mortar wounds to the torso and legs at the Battle of Khe Sanh. I remember the day my parents received the telegram about the death of their nephew **Donald Van der Schans**. Life turned upside down for the family then. Everyone was very sad, especially when we went to Arlington Memorial Cemetery in Arlington, Virginia, to participate in the burial ceremony for Donald.

Many years later, when I was in my forties, I went to visit Donald's grave with my children. I often wondered why my Aunt Virginia (Ginny) died less than a year after her son was killed in Vietnam. Perhaps the death of Donald was too much for her to bear. My mother said she died of a "broken heart."

Grave marker for Donald Edward Van Der Schans, with our sons Alex and Andy beside it

Genealogy is about uncovering the past, be it good, bad, or awful. With the Zealand family line there certainly was a lot of awful, but I bet you it was mixed in with much good too. There are certainly many hundreds of Zealands out there descending from the English immigrant Edward William Zealand Sr. I know I have Zealand relatives living in Canada, the US, and New Zealand, and possibly other countries too. Judging from the happy family photos and detailed biographical information on Zealand family members I've seen and included in my Ancestry family tree, it can't have been all bad times.

Despite the terrible blows life dealt the Zealands, if you look back into your own family history, you will undoubtedly see that your ancestors had to face similar, if not worse, situations. All we can do in the face of this certain knowledge is continue living, loving, and laughing until the end comes for us.

Surprises May Be in Store

As you can see, being a genealogist can help you uncover amazing facts about your ancestors. One surprise I learned, as already mentioned while growing my tree, was that Stephen Hopkins was my great-grandfather eleven generations ago. He came to the British Colonies in 1620, arriving in Massachusetts on the *Mayflower*. He was a founding member of the Massachusetts Bay Colony and one of the signatories of the Mayflower Compact. I also learned, as I conducted more research, that Hopkins liked to hold parties where people drank alcohol. He got in trouble with the law on more than one occasion for having these parties and for charging too much for alcoholic beverages.

Hopkins and his descendants were an interesting family. *Mayflower* passenger **Giles Hopkins**, son of Stephen Hopkins, had a daughter, **Deborah Hopkins**, born in 1648 in Barnstable, Massachusetts. In 1668, when she was twenty, she married **Josias Cooke**. Records from that time show that Josias got into a fight and was injured. Later he sued a man for a debt of four pounds and won a judgment of three pounds. He also sued someone named John Smith from Plymouth for slander, and John Smith agreed that he had "much wronged the plaintiff by his unbridled tongue in these base and false charges."

Despite his legal issues, Josias managed to have seven children with his wife Deborah Hopkins. The oldest of Josias's seven children, **Elizabeth Cooke**, also settled in Barnstable. She married **Thomas Newcomb** and they had three children, including **Deborah Newcomb**, born in 1702 in Truro, Massachusetts. This area is a popular tourist destination just south of the northern tip of Cape Cod, not far from Provincetown, Massachusetts.

Deborah Newcomb married **Thomas Lamkin**. Together they moved from Massachusetts to Connecticut. They had a daughter named **Mary Lamkin**, who lived from 1732 to 1790. Her husband, **Archippus Blodgett**, was a soldier in the American Revolution. From

Archippus, a Revolutionary War soldier, who died in 1790, to me, Nancy Blodgett, born in 1956, there is an unbroken line of Blodgetts for nine generations. This is how *Mayflower* passenger Stephen Hopkins is related to me.

I was also able to verify this connection by checking on the LDS site FamilySearch. It has a tree in it called *Community Trees – Mayflower Pilgrim Genealogies*. It showed a direct link from Stephen Hopkins–Giles Hopkins–Deborah Hopkins–Elizabeth Cooke–Deborah Newcomb to Mary Lamkin, who married Archippus Blodgett in 1753. They are my great-grandparents six generations back.

This couple had at least seven children. Unfortunately, the existing FamilySearch Mayflower Pilgrim Genealogies doesn't include all the siblings. It only includes Elijah, Josiah, and Mary Blodgett and their spouses. But their brother Henry Blodgett, born May 14, 1767, in Stratford, New Hampshire, is definitely a member of this family. He is my great-grandfather five generations ago. I tried to update this tree but was unable to do so as it doesn't currently offer this option. Fortunately, FamilySearch does acknowledge that Stephen Hopkins is my great-grandfather eleven generations back. Using at least two different genealogy websites is a must if you want to verify the facts on your tree.

Another surprise I discovered while growing my tree is that I have a famous French cousin named **Philip De Lannoy**, from Leiden, in the Netherlands. His mother was **Marie Mahieu**. She was born in 1580 in Canterbury, England, to a Protestant English mother and French father. From 1562 to 1598, a religious struggle called the Wars of Religion took place between Catholics and French Protestants, known as Huguenots, who supported the ideas of John Calvin. Since the French royalty supported the Catholics, this led to brutal conflicts against Protestants, causing many of them to flee to England.

Historians estimated two to four million people died during these wars. One of the worst events occurred August 23, 1572, when approximately seventy thousand Huguenots were killed by Catholics in what is now known as the St. Bartholomew's Day Massacre. After this happened, a huge number of Huguenots left France and went to England and Holland. This great conflict didn't get resolved until the Edict of Nantes was signed in 1598, giving the Huguenots equal rights to Catholics.

England was a Protestant nation and encouraged these Huguenot refugees to come live there. Many were skilled craftsmen, including weavers. A church was founded in Canterbury in 1561 for them. These religious refugees also lived in London, Norwich, and Southampton, where many more houses of worship were established. Between 1560 and 1570 the estimated number of refugees in England was between six thousand and seven thousand people.

In Canterbury, in particular, the population grew substantially, with an estimated two thousand French Protestant refugees there during this period. Protestantism was already well established in this city. King Edward VI allowed these refugees to worship in the western crypt of Canterbury Cathedral. This chapel, Église Protestante Française de Cantorbéry, is still in use today.

Since Canterbury was crowded with religious refugees, it may have been difficult for everyone to earn a living. Perhaps this is part of the reason the De Lannoy family moved to Leiden, in the Netherlands, around 1590. Leiden had a reputation for being tolerant of people of different faiths.

Phillip De Lannoy, my sixth cousin fourteen generations removed, was born in Leiden in 1602, not long after the *Edict of Nantes* was signed. When he was eighteen, he decided to sail to the colonies on a ship called the Fortune. He arrived at Plymouth, Massachusetts, on November 9, 1621. He was the first Huguenot to settle in the colonies and leave American descendants, including Franklin Delano Roosevelt.

Like other settlers to America, De Lannoy may have decided to come to what would one day become the United States to worship freely, without being told what to believe by government authorities.

And like other early settlers, his life was probably very hard, especially with the brutal Massachusetts winters. Between 1620 and 1640, twenty thousand English men, women, and children crossed the Atlantic Ocean to settle New England in what is called "the Great Migration."

One of my relatives who took part in the Great Migration was Thomas Blodgett. I mentioned him earlier. He came on the ship Increase from England to Boston in 1635. He, his wife Susanna, and their two sons, Daniel and Samuel, are all mentioned on page 61 in the book *The Original List of Persons of Quality 1600–1700*. Samuel, my great-grandfather ten generations back, wasn't even two years old at the time! To be able to make the trip, they had to bring along certificates from the minister and their justice of the peace that attested to their conformity to the Church of England. Not just anybody could go to the colonies. One had to prove oneself worthy as well as have enough money to afford the trip across the Atlantic Ocean.

Once they arrived in Massachusetts after a seven-week voyage, **Thomas Blodgett**, originally from Stowmarket, in Suffolk, England, decided to settle himself and his family in Newtown. This city was later named Cambridge. Even though he had listed his profession as a glove maker on the passenger manifest, he decided to try farming. He had property both in the town center and on the edge of "cow common." This place where cows grazed later became Harvard University! According to a Blodgett family historian, the place where Thomas and his wife's farm stood would later become part of the grounds of the Harvard Observatory. This is now known as the Harvard Smithsonian Center for Astrophysics. This is the kind of interesting bit of historical information that makes genealogy so fun.

Moving ahead to 1775, long past the Great Migration, about 2.5 million people traveled to North America. As already mentioned, many people migrated to America for religious freedom. But many others came for better economic opportunities or to get away from conflicts in their native countries, just as people are still doing today. Later on, wars were fought in America too, between the new settlers and Native Americans, and then the Revolutionary War between the colonists and the British. Stephen Hopkins, son Giles, and their descendants had family members who fought in the American Revolution.

And speaking of wars, while growing my tree I learned that **Winston Churchill**, the Prime Minister of England during World War II, is my seventh cousin, two generations removed. His mother, **Jeanette "Jennie" Jerome**, was American, having been born in Brooklyn, New York, in 1854. Her great-great-grandfather was **Samuel Jerome**, born in Wallingford, Connecticut, in 1728. He is my second cousin, seven generations removed.

Another famous relative I was pleased to have a connection to was **Sir Francis Bacon**. He is my first cousin, thirteen generations removed, as we share the same great-grandfather. That is **Anthony Cooke**, who was famous in his own right. He served as the High Sheriff of Essex, England, in 1545. At King Edward VI's coronation, Anthony Cooke was created a Knight of the Bath, an important honor. He was also a humanist scholar and tutor to King Edward VI.

His daughter, **Ann Cooke**, mother of Francis Bacon, was highly educated and a published author. In 1550, when she was just twenty-two years old, "she translated and published Bernardino Uchino's work *Ochinos's Sermons* from the Italian." Apparently, she also had strong opinions about religion and was sympathetic to Puritan positions of the day. She wrote many letters to clergymen at the time, debating her theological views with them and quoting classical Greek and Latin authors to support her opinions.

Her son Francis Bacon was more famous than his mother or grandfather. He was a philosopher and served as both Attorney General and Lord Chancellor under King James I of England. He is considered the father of empiricism, and I studied his ideas in college as I majored in philosophy. Empiricism is the idea that true knowledge or evidence for one's beliefs can only come from sensory observation. Ideas one holds must be supported by evidence, not just opinions.

My great-grandmother twelve generations back is **Mildred Cooke**, Francis Bacon's aunt. Older sister to Ann Cooke, she was well-educated and worked as a translator. She had an impressive library of books, mainly in Latin and Greek. She also married well. Her husband was William Cecil, reportedly the most-trusted advisor to Queen Elizabeth I. So that's an accomplished group of people!

Another big surprise I learned while growing my tree is that my great-grandaunt **Philippa Roet**, born in 1350 in Picardy, France, was married to **Geoffrey Chaucer**, the famous English author, poet, and civil servant. His most famous work was *The Canterbury Tales*. Philippa's father, **Paon de Roet**, my great-grandfather seventeen generations ago, was ancestor to many kings of England and Scotland.

I was initially astonished to learn I was related to many kings and queens of England, Scotland, France, and even Spain. But I now gather that's not particularly unusual, especially if you have ancestors who came over from Europe to the British (later to become American) colonies in the 1600s.

Are You Related to Royalty Too?

You will discover that the further back you go on your tree, the more you will find "pedigree collapse." That would be, for example, first cousins marrying each other, thus reducing the number of ancestors that exist before them. Children of first cousins who married would only have six great-grandparents rather than the more typical eight. This happens a lot with royals as ancestors, reducing the total expected number of people you can be related to as you go back in time. As a result, more of the same people will keep showing up on different branches of your tree the further back you go. Indeed, I read if we go back one thousand years in Europe, everyone will have the same set of ancestors, so that they will all be descendants of William the Conqueror, who was born in Burgundy, France, around 1020.

According to many genealogists, most of the European population is related to William the Conqueror, as are countless Americans of British ancestry. So don't think you are super special if you can link yourself back to him. Especially don't post selfies of you with paintings of him and load them onto Ancestry!

Since I have more than 50 percent British/Scottish ancestry, I was able to link my tree back to this famous man. William the Conqueror is my great-grandfather twenty-five generations back, according to census records. His son **Henry I, King of England**, was my great-grandfather twenty-four generations ago. This king was known as "Beauclerc" as well as the "Lion of Justice." For all the good works he may have done, he died in 1135 in Normandy, France, from eating too many eels. Most unfortunate. One must not go overboard eating eels.

Henry I's daughter was **Matilda Beauclerk**. She married **Geoffrey V Plantagenet** when she was twenty-six years old and he was only fifteen. They didn't get along at first, partly due to the age difference. She had previously been married to Henry V, the Holy Roman Emperor and a man thirty years older than her. But he died before they could have any children. After this second match, there were Plantagenets from then on for many generations. That's one of the main names appearing on my tree of nine thousand people. These kings and queens had big families and married other royals, so if you do have one king or queen as a relative, I bet you have a dozen or more if you start looking.

Matilda Beauclerk gave birth to **King Henry II Plantagenet** of England in 1133. He was known as Curtmantle Plantagenet. He married **Eleanor of Aquitaine** in 1152 and they proceeded to have a great number of Plantagenet children. One of their daughters, Eleanor Plantagenet, is my great-grandmother twenty-two generations back. She married the Spanish **King Alfonso VIII** of Castille, so I have many Spanish kings as great-grandparents.

King Henry II and his wife Eleanor of Aquitaine had a son known as **John Lackland I**, King of England. He is my great-grandfather twenty-one generations ago. John Lackland is related to almost every president of the United States too, according to media reports.

Even though having royals as relatives is not unique, it certainly is exciting. It also makes me motivated to learn more about the history of that time period. One thing I have noticed while researching this time in history is how many grandfathers died in battle. My goodness, this happened a lot. It happened so much that I created a new tree tag in Ancestry called Killed in Battle. I added this tag to all my grandfathers who were killed in famous European battles. History doesn't have to be something impersonal and abstract. When you become a genealogist, it can be very personal and meaningful, especially if it's your relatives who fought and died. Let me tell you about some of them and the battles they fought in. Some of these men might be your relatives too.

Lots of Killing

Malcolm III, King of Scotland

Going back very far, let's talk about **Malcolm Canmore III**, King of Scotland. My great-grandfather twenty-five generations back, he was born in 1031 in Perthshire, Scotland. This relative was nicknamed Canmore. In Gaelic, this means "big head." According to the Dictionary of National Biography, "Malcolm was almost incessantly engaged in wars." This entry on my relative also said he couldn't read but did speak Latin, English, and Gaelic. His wife, **Margaret of Wessex**, Queen of Scotland, was, by contrast, quite cultured and religious. Indeed she was so pious and did so many charitable works that she was later canonized in 1250 by the Pope.

Malcolm was killed by an army of knights led by Robert de Mowbray on November 13, 1093, at the Battle of Alnwick in Northumberland, England, while his eldest son Edward died from battle wounds a few days later. Apparently Malcolm III wanted to control Northumbria, but Mowbray, who was actually the Earl of Northumbria, wasn't keen on this possibility. He and his men surprised my grandfather and his oldest son near Alnwick Castle. Grandmother Margaret died of grief a few days after hearing the news about the death of her husband and oldest child.

The Unfortunate Percy Family

Shortly before and during the War of the Roses, many male Percy relatives were killed. **Lord Henry Percy**—the son of the first Earl of Northumberland, **Henry Percy**, and his wife **Margaret Neville**—was born May 20, 1364, in Northumberland, England. His nickname was "Hotspur." With a name like that, he already sounds like trouble. He is my great-grandfather nineteen generations ago, according to Ancestry records.

He was an English knight who fought against the Scots and later against the French during the Hundred Years' War. He undertook military and diplomatic activities in support of King Richard II. However, he and his father decided to support Henry Bolingbrook, Henry IV, in his rebellion against King Richard II. This worked out for them when King Richard was deposed and they were rewarded with more land and political offices. Even so, both father and son grew discontented with King Henry. For example, he didn't pay them the wages they thought were due them for defending England's border against attacks by the Scots, nor did he give them promised lands, among other grievances. So in 1403 the Percy family decided to fight the king. This worked out fine for them the time they rebelled against King Richard II, so maybe it would work again?

Hotspur decided to attack the Prince of Wales, later known as Henry V, the son of current King Henry IV, at Shrewsbury. Henry Hotspur Percy was supposed to meet an army led by his father there so they could fight together. However, Hotspur and his men got there first and found the king had assembled a huge army to meet him. Hotspur's uncle, **Thomas Percy**, first Earl of Worcester, was also there to battle the current king. At the Battle of Shrewsbury, Hotspur Henry was killed. Some historians report he was shot in the face by an arrow when he opened his visor. His uncle was captured at the battle and was beheaded in Shrewsbury two days later, on July 23, 1403.

Here is a painting shared on Ancestry depicting the scene of my relative's death.

Hotspur's father didn't participate in the battle so wasn't convicted of treason. However, he continued to have disputes with the king and was killed at the Battle of Branham Moor on February 20, 1408.

Hotspur's son, **Henry Percy,** second Earl of Northumberland, my great-grandfather eighteen generations back, was also killed in battle. He died May 22, 1455, at the Battle of St. Albans, considered the first battle of the War of the Roses. He was an English nobleman and military commander, like his father, but he served on the side of the king. At that time, the King of England was Henry VI, who was taken captive by forces loyal to the Duke of York while Henry Percy was killed in battle. Henry's son, also called Henry, third Earl of Northumberland, was also killed in battle. He was my great-uncle seventeen generations ago, according to Ancestry records, and he died at the Battle of Towton in March 1461. This War of the Roses battle was reportedly the "largest and bloodiest battle" in English soil up to that point. Uncle Henry was fighting on the Lancastrian side of the war against the Yorkists. The Yorkists won the battle and Edward IV became king, deposing the Lancastrian Henry VI. As I mentioned earlier, lots of deaths in battle among my family members. Special shout-out goes to the Percy family, though, who probably had the most family members killed among my ancestors.

Feuding Among Scottish Relatives

As mentioned earlier, I am 51% Scottish according to my Ancestry DNA results. It's amazing how spitting into a vial and sending it off to a laboratory can result in so much specific information. Not only am I more than half Scottish, but much of my family comes from the Scottish Highlands and Islands, and specifically from the Ross and Cromarty region. Now that's specific! I am also 34% English and Northwestern European, 12% Irish, 2% Germanic Empire, and 1% Swedish/Danish. According to Ancestry, they assessed my DNA against eighteen hundred different regions in the world. That sounds pretty thorough to me. And all for only one hundred dollars.

Anyway, let's talk about my Scottish ancestors. These guys really liked to get into fights with other clans or with the English. Let's go back to **Robert Stewart II**, born March 2, 1316. He was the first Monarch of the House of Stewarts and was my second cousin twenty-one generations removed. He was King of Scotland from 1371 until his death in 1390. His parents were **Walter Stewart**, sixth High Stewart of Scotland, and **Marjorie Bruce**, the daughter of **Robert the Bruce**, King of the Scots. Walter Stewart reportedly found time to have twenty-one children to two wives and several mistresses. One of his children, **Robert III**, became king upon his death. According to Independence and Nationhood by Alexander Grant, son Robert III "was probably Scotland's least impressive king."

But to be honest, it didn't seem like his father did very much in terms of accomplishments either, with his kingship said to be "nominal." As for Robert III, Abbot Walter Bower reported that this Scottish king described himself as "the worst of kings and the most miserable of men." Not the most impressive of relatives. Apparently during his reign there was much fighting and anarchy, and he was supposedly unable to control his brothers Albany and Buchan or his son Rothesay. Author Ranald Nicholson wrote in his book *Scotland: The Later Middle Ages* that Robert III was a failure, just like his father, because they didn't have assertive personalities as kings must have to reign over their subjects.

The grandfather of King Robert II was Robert the Bruce, my great-granduncle twenty-one generations ago. He actually accomplished some important things when he was the leader of Scotland. He freed Scotland from English rule in 1314, winning the famous Battle of Bannockburn. Scottish independence was ratified in the 1328 signing of the Treaty of Northampton. The great-grandson of Robert the Bruce was **James I Stewart**, King of Scotland, my fourth cousin nineteen generations removed, who married **Joan Beaufort**, my great-grandmother fourteen generations back. After he was killed in 1437, Joan waited two years and then married another man, also named James Stewart. This relative was known as the Black Knight of Lorne, my fourteenth great-grandfather. According to the book, *The Royal Stuarts: A History of the Family that Shaped Britain*, Joan made a mistake in choosing her second husband. The book's author, Allan Massie, writes that "The mistake lay less in the fact of remarriage, for that was expected of widows, than in her choice of husband. Sir James Stewart, a distant royal cousin, was a wild and ambitious man with an unsavoury reputation."

He might have been "unsavoury" (or "unsavory" as Americans would spell it), but he didn't get killed like her first husband. Joan Beaufort and the Black Knight of Lorne had a son in 1439 named **John**

Stewart, the first Earl of Atholl. Two of his children, **John Stewart**, second Earl of Atholl, and his sister, **Catherine Stewart**, are my great-grandparents as well. He is twelve generations back while she is thirteen generations back.

The King of Scotland's son, **James Stewart II**, was also killed. He died in 1460 at the siege of Roxburgh Castle, one of the last castles still held by the English after Scottish independence. King James II led a campaign to capture this castle from the English while they were distracted by the War of the Roses. It didn't work out so well for my great-uncle, though, as he was standing too close to a cannon he had ordered to be fired and was killed. His son, **King James Stewart III**, didn't have much better luck. He inherited the throne upon the death of his father, but he was only a child. According to historians, even as he grew up, he wasn't popular or effective. Because of his unpopular policies and ineffective rule, he made a lot of enemies. Ultimately, nobles who opposed him fought those who supported him at the Battle of Sauchieburn. This was fought June 11, 1488, near the city of Stirling in central Scotland. Historians are unclear how King James III died at this battle. He was my great-grandfather sixteen generations ago.

James III's son, **King James Stewart IV** of Scotland, was also killed. He died on September 9, 1513, at Flodden Field. This James was killed in yet another battle between England and Scotland. It was the largest battle ever fought between these two kingdoms. James IV was killed in the fighting, just like his father. Maybe the Stewart family can rival the Percy family for number of family members killed in battle!

In the battle of Flodden Field, historians claim between ten thousand and seventeen thousand Scottish men were killed, including a large number of Scottish nobles along with their king, while the English were said to have lost only about fifteen hundred men. Although many historians mark this battle as the end of the Middle Ages, it certainly wasn't the end of the fighting. There were many Scottish clan feuds during the 1500s.

Two of the most awful clan battles took place in 1577 and 1578. The feud in 1577 took place on the Isle of Eigg between the McLeods and the McDonalds. The year before that, the whole population of Eigg was destroyed after the McLeods suffocated more than 350 McDonalds in a cave after lighting a fire at the cave's opening. The trigger for this catastrophe was when three McLeod men had been cast adrift in a boat after insulting some young Eigg women. The McLeods wanted to avenge the ill treatment of their men.

A year later, a feud between the McLeods and McDonalds erupted at a church in Skye. Members of the McDonald clan surrounded a church and set fire to it, killing almost everyone inside. Apparently one woman escaped through a window and alerted her McLeod family. Those that weren't in the church arrived and killed all the McDonalds who were there.

Ian, one of the members of my writers' group in Spain, is from Scotland. He remarked that "the only time the clans came together was to fight the English." Otherwise, they would just fight each other. This was the nature of the clan system.

MacLeod and McDonald are two of the three clan names that regularly appear in the Scottish branches of my tree. In my tree currently, there are at least forty-seven people with the surname MacLeod and twelve with the name McLeod. Both names are pronounced MacCloud. The clan motto for the MacLeods is "Hold fast." Clan MacLeod has its ancestral home on the Isle of Skye. Supposedly this clan descended from Norse kings in the thirteenth century. They have been in Scotland for a long time.

Twenty-five people have the last name of MacDonald in my tree. Their motto is "By sea and by land." They were apparently one of the largest clans in the Scottish Highlands. Many of them lived around Glencoe, a village in western Scotland.

A third well-known Scottish clan name that appears in my tree is MacKenzie. Twenty-two people in my tree have the last name of

MacKenzie. Their motto is "I shine, not burn." This is one of the best-known clans in Scotland. They lived on the Isle of Lewis as well as in Western Ross and Cromarty, known as Wester Ross, and in Easter Ross. This part of the Scottish Highlands is northwest of Inverness.

Uncovering Good and Bad Relatives

While scouring your family tree for information, you are likely to find both heroes and villains among your relatives in addition to people who have been killed. If you are going back more than a few generations, the discovery of a family tragedy isn't so personal, like the earlier painful story of my Zealand relatives, but more likely just confirmation that there are good people in the world and bad people. Both might be your relatives.

I discovered that my Deland granduncle three generations back worked on the Underground Railroad, for example. His name was **Hall Deland** and he was born August 9, 1796, in Massachusetts. He later moved to Bedford, Monroe County, Michigan. Census records show he lived there in 1840, 1850, and 1860, all before the start of the Civil War. This is where he was living when he helped slaves cross into Canada to freedom. (Even though census records can be inaccurate at times, especially concerning spelling of names, looking at them is a great way to help verify some of the facts of your tree.)

Hall was called "The Nighthawk." According to one of Hall's sons, his father helped many male and female slaves escape to freedom as they passed through Bedford in Monroe County, Ohio. Apparently Hall, who worked as a farmer, had a wagon built with a false bottom where he would hide the slaves and then put bags of grain or hay on top of the false floor to keep them safe. Supposedly, my great-uncle escorted the slaves at nighttime to French settlers living by the Detroit River who then brought them across the border into Canada. Wow, Uncle Hall. You rock! That was so courageous of you.

Apparently, helping slaves escape to freedom was a family tree for the Delands. Another ancestor doing this was William Rufus Deland. He was a second cousin to Hall Deland as their grandfathers were both sons of **Paul Deland**. William is my second cousin five generations removed.

According to a website about the Underground Railroad that operated in Jackson, Michigan, **William Rufus Deland** used his home from the 1830s to 1865 as a station for slaves to stay on their way to freedom in Canada. Born in 1795 in Massachusetts, he later migrated with his family to Michigan. He was one of the first settlers to Jackson and was its first justice of the peace. He also started a newspaper called The American Citizen and was a co-founder of one of the town's first churches, the first Congregational Church of Jackson.

William Rufus Deland

Historians write that his wife, Mary Green Keith, helped encourage her family to participate in helping slaves to freedom and she helped feed and care for these secret visitors. William Rufus Deland Their oldest son, Charles Victor Deland, wrote that as a youth he often drove his father's lumber wagon, with slaves hidden in the back, to the next station on the Underground Railroad. Charles also fought in the Civil War and was promoted to a Colonel of the First Sharpshooters of Michigan. He was wounded several times in the war, including the December 1862 Battle of Murfreesboro, Tennessee, where he was captured by the enemy and spent five months in prison. Here is a photo of Charles taken during the Civil War.

Col. Charles Victor Deland

Col. Charles Victor Deland Charles later became editor of *The American Citizen* where he used the paper to campaign against slavery. He also wrote and published a history of Jackson County, Michigan.

If any of these ancestors had been caught helping slaves, they could have been sent to jail for up to six months and fined $1,000, an enormous sum back in the 1800s. Thank you brave ancestors! You knew slavery was wrong and you actively opposed it at risk to your own livelihood.

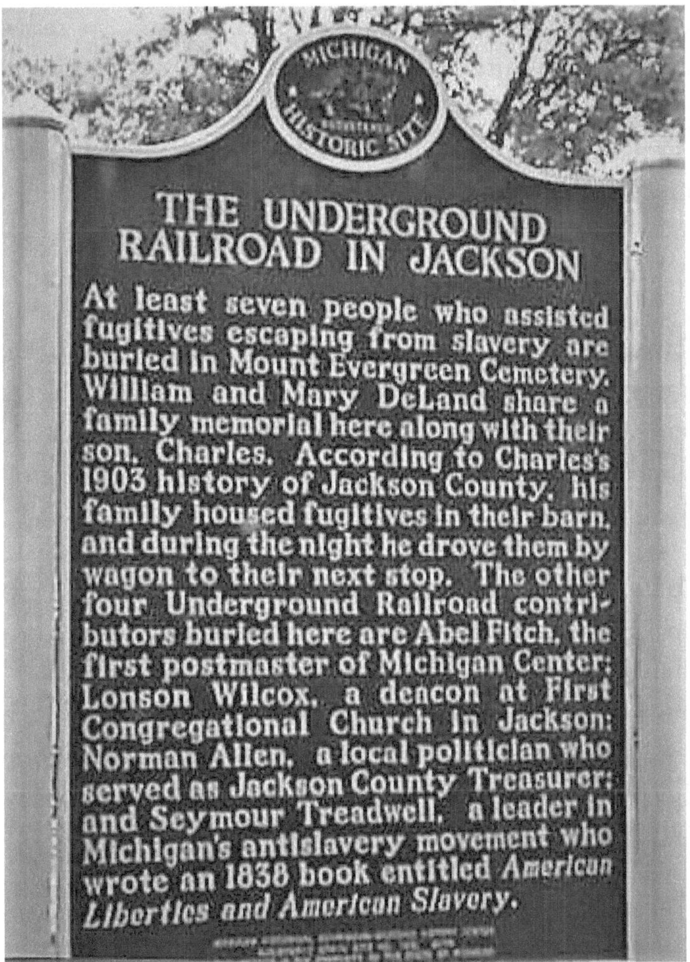

Charles, his father and mother were honored by Jackson County with a cemetery plaque.

Now on to a relative I am not so proud of. My great-grandmother four generations ago on my father's side was named **Nancy Mary Morgan.** She was born April 11, 1795, in New Hampshire. Later, she married **Zebina Blodgett** in 1818, most likely in Vermont, where they raised their children together. Her older brother, **Oliver Jones Morgan**, was also born in New Hampshire, on May 23, 1784. But in his twenties, he moved to Louisiana and married a local woman there on May 12, 1817. While living in Ouachita, Louisiana, with his wife, Narcissa Deeson White, he owned hundreds of slaves. Census records report him living in Ouachita in 1810, 1820, and 1830. In 1850, a US census was done of his slaves. He had also moved to Carroll Parish by this time. When my great uncle died in 1860, just before the start of the Civil War, he owned the following according to public records related to his estate:

> Inventory of the estate of the deceased Oliver J. Morgan, involving an extremely large amount of land; 353 slaves ranging in age from infancy to 74 years, equipment, animals, and utensils, valued at $1,182,314.80, located in Carroll Parish.

He had 353 slaves ranging from infancy to seventy-four years old. That makes me so sad! According to public records, he was one of the wealthiest slave-owners in Carroll Parish in Louisiana.

This is what the local newspaper, *The Ouachita Telegraph*, had to say about him on November 19, 1860, after his death. This information was also published on Oliver Morgan's record on the Find A Grave site.

THE LATE OLIVER J. MORGAN.

> The remains of the late Judge OLIVER J. MORGAN, who died on his plantation in the parish of Carroll, October 5th, 1860, were reinterred Sunday last in the family burying-ground on the Limerick Plantation, on the Bayou DeSiard, by the Masonic Order. He was at one time Senior Warden of Western Star Lodge, No. 24, and as such, was buried with highest honors of the Order. A large number of citizens did honor by their presence to the mortal remains of this esteemed brother.

Judge Morgan was born in Connecticut in 1793. His parents moved to Boston, Mass., while he was an infant. He came to Louisiana when a young man and was Parish Judge of the parish of Ouachita for many years. Full of energy and financial ability, he engaged in planting and became one of the wealthiest and most respected citizens. For a number of years he resided on his plantation on Bayou DeSiard, from which he moved to Carroll parish and opened several large plantations on the alluvial lands of the Mississippi river where he lived until he died.

Few men have been more financially successful than he was. Starting with very limited means, he accumulated a large amount of property. His character was of noble type, and his generosity large as his ability. He understood the energy and progress of this age, and deeply felt the necessity of guiding it into the proper channels. Hence he was liberal in his donations to all institutions designed to benefit and educate the masses. To the University of the South he gave forty thousand dollars. His death was a sad loss to the country in which he lived, and a calamity to his relations and friends, but, we hope, a blessing to himself in that happy land from which no brother is willing to return. —By resolve of Western Star Lodge No. 24. November 6th, 1870.

Apparently, views differ on whether my great-uncle was a good person or a terrible one. Yes, he helped the community and donated money to good causes, but he enslaved Black people for many years on his plantations.

False Accusations of Witchcraft

Many actions or types of behavior done by ancestors can be subject to a negative interpretation that may be fully justified or might not be true at all. For instance, at least two of my grandmothers were accused of witchcraft. One of them lived during the War of the Roses and the other was alive during the time of the Salem Witch Trials. Both women appeared to have strong personalities and no fear of sharing their strong opinions with others. This behavior alone probably caused problems for them both, given the time periods and places in which they lived.

Elizabeth Woodville

Elizabeth Woodville of England was my great-grandmother fifteen generations ago. She became famous when she married King Edward IV of England in secret on May 1, 1464. Because she wasn't of royal birth, she was immediately disliked by many people in the royal court. Some people also said that King Edward and Elizabeth's marriage only came about "by Sorcerie and Wichecrafte, committed by the said Elizabeth, and her Moder (mother) Jaquett Duchess of Bedford." She also came from a family of Lancastrian supporters, while King Edward IV was on the Yorkist side during the War of the Roses. Her first husband, John Grey of Groby, was killed at the second battle of St. Albans, fighting on the Lancastrian side. So this match was seen as wrong in many people's eyes. After they were married, her brother-in-law, the king's brother, George of Clarence, reportedly accused her of witchcraft in the untimely death of his wife, Isabel Neville, after childbirth.

Apparently, Woodville also caused offense to many people by appointing her relatives to high office and giving some of them noble titles. Nepotism never goes over very well in any age.

After her husband King Edward IV died in April 1483, Richard III, one of her husband's other brothers, accused her of witchcraft too. He also accused her of plotting to "murder and utterly destroy" him. After this, Richard had her son by her first marriage, Richard Grey, and her brother Anthony Woodville, executed. In addition, her son Edward, who was supposed to be King Edward V, and his younger brother Richard, were locked up in the Tower of London on the authority of their uncle and were never seen again after the summer of 1483. This is the famous Princes in the Tower story that is a mystery to this day. Poor lady.

Elizabeth Hutchinson

Elizabeth Hutchinson was born in 1620 in Lynn, Massachusetts. She was my great-grandmother only nine generations ago. Her father and mother had both immigrated from England. She was raised in that area and married a farmer named Isaac Hart. Elizabeth Hutchinson Hart was accused of witchcraft when she was an old woman. According to the book *The Salem Witch Trials: A Day-by-Day Chronicle of a Community Under Siege* by Marilynne Roach, Elizabeth Hart "was bold enough to have confronted Ann Putnam Jr. directly when the girl accused her of witchcraft and outspoken enough that the Lynn Church had reprimanded her in 1655 for calling her fellow members 'fools and lackwits.'" Clearly, this is a woman who speaks her mind. Despite her protestations, she was jailed in May of 1662 for tormenting Mary Warren, one of the accusers. Imprisoned in Boston for almost seven months, she was only released after repeated pleas were made to the court from her son Thomas Hart. She was lucky, too, because later on, between 1692 and 1693, the Salem Witch Trials took place. More than two hundred people were accused of practicing witchcraft, and nineteen of them were executed by hanging. Fourteen of those hanged were women.

To me it sounds like some people just thought my relatives, Elizabeth Woodville and Elizabeth Hutchinson, were difficult people, and they wanted to get them in trouble by calling them witches. It turns out that in addition to speaking one's mind by calling people "fools and lackwits," female relatives got themselves in trouble by dressing in a way that was out of the ordinary. My great-grandmother Thomasine Boyes, married to Rev. Francis Johnson, got harassed by other people, including her brother-in-law George Johnson, when she didn't dress in a plain and simple manner. Indeed, George was afraid that his brother Francis was "blinded, bewitched, and besotted" by this "proud woman," and he considered it his duty as a good Christian to help reform the situation. Notice the use of the word "bewitched." Was she witchlike because she wanted to be a fashionable dresser? I will talk more about Thomasine in the next section on religious leaders escaping persecution for their ideas.

Religious Leaders Flee Oppression

Another thing you will be likely to uncover if you are a genealogist is that you have relatives with a religious connection among some or maybe all of your family's lines. I have at least twenty-one male relatives who were clergy members in England or the Thirteen Colonies. Many of these ancestors left their country of birth in the 1620s and 1630s. In fact, beginning at the start of this period as many as twenty thousand people left England to worship as they pleased in America. Charles I was King of England, Scotland, and Ireland from March 27, 1625, until his execution in 1649. Charles encouraged the Catholic bishops to enforce compliance with Anglican Church practices and encouraged the suspension of those who refused to adhere to the style of worship dictated by The Book of Common Prayer. There were other disagreements on how to worship God and what needed to be in a church, such as altar rails or not, that caused conflict as well.

One of my minister relatives who left England during this time frame for more freedom to worship in a way of his choosing was **Rev. John Lothrop**. He was my great-grandfather ten generations back. He was born in Yorkshire, England, on December 20, 1584. As an adult, he served as a pastor of a Congregational church teaching the New Testament. He and many of his congregation were imprisoned in England for their beliefs for two years beginning on April 29, 1632. Sadly, his first wife died while he was in prison.

Finally, he and some of his congregants were allowed to be freed as long as they agreed to leave the country. He sailed with others to Massachusetts on September 18, 1634, with a second wife. Shortly thereafter, he organized a church in Scituate, Massachusetts. Later on, he founded a church in Barnstable, Massachusetts. He had at least eight children, including my great-grandfather, **Samuel Lathrop**, born in 1623 in Kent, England, and dying in New London, Connecticut, in 1700.

Another minister relative, born eight years before John Lothrop, was **Rev. John Robinson**. Born in 1576 in Sturton-le-Steeple, Nottinghamshire, England, he was my great-grandfather eleven generations ago. Like Lothrop, he wasn't keen on the way the Anglican Church was practicing the Christian faith. He joined a group of ministers called the Scrooby Separatists. They met at the Scrooby, England, home of William Brewster. (Brewster would later become a Mayflower passenger and leader of the Plymouth Colony.) In 1607, members of this group tried to escape England from the city of Boston, also in England, but were betrayed. Rev. Robinson ended up in prison in Boston Guildhall for his religious beliefs. Luckily after his trial, he was freed, while some members of the Separatists then successfully fled to Amsterdam. They later moved to Leiden, where Rev. Robinson joined the group in 1609. Robinson became the pastor of the church there. He was recognized as a leading scholar of the Separatist movement, authoring many books about his religious views. He was also one of the planners of the Separatists' (Pilgrims') trip to America on the *Mayflower*.

Even though Leiden was a tolerant place that allowed people to worship freely, historians say many English people who had fled there because of religious persecution worried that their children were becoming more Dutch than English. Since they didn't want this to happen, they decided to start over in America. Some people also worried about the ongoing conflict between Holland and Spain, another Catholic country. If Spain were to decisively win this war, then the Separatists would need to leave again. (This war first started in 1568 and didn't end until 1648. It was later referred to as the Eighty Years' War).

When some of the members of Robinson's religious congregation were about to leave for the Colonies on the *Mayflower* in 1620, Robinson gave the service for them. He planned to join them when a second wave of Pilgrims was to come over. But he died before he could do that. He was buried under his St. Pieterkirk Church on March 4, 1625. A plaque honoring him is there. It states about him:

> His broadly tolerant mind guided and developed the religious life of the Pilgrims of the *Mayflower*. Of him these walls enshrine all that was mortal. His undying Spirit still dominates the consciences of a mighty nation in the land beyond the seas.

Son Isaac Robinson sailed from Leiden to Massachusetts in 1631 on the ship *Lion*. He was twenty-one years old at the time. His father John had died six years earlier. Isaac Robinson has many American descendants, including me.

Another relative who fled England because of religious persecution was **Rev. John Wilson**, born in Windsor, England, in 1588, four years after Rev. John Lathrop's birth. Like the two other relatives I mentioned, Rev. Wilson left his native land for America in 1630 because of his religious views. He sailed across the Atlantic Ocean with his friend John Winthrop. John Wilson was my great-grandfather ten generations back. Once in America, he became a Puritan clergyman in Boston in the Massachusetts Bay Colony. Later, he was minister of the First Church of Boston from its establishment in Charlestown in 1630 until his death in 1667. Coming to Massachusetts didn't solve his problems, however, and he got caught up in a religious controversy with Ann Hutchinson and her brother-in-law Rev. John Wheelwright. They had a sharp disagreement with Wilson over elements of faith, such as whether one could receive salvation through good works (Wilson's view) versus by faith (Hutchinson and Wheelwright's view). In 1637, a trial took place, and Wheelwright was banished from the church for his views. Hutchinson was also tried for her views, which the court considered "theological errors."

She was ultimately excommunicated, and Rev. Wilson reportedly said the following to her at the end of the trial:

The Church consentinge to it we will proced to excommunication forasmuch as you, Mrs. Hutchinson, have highly transgressed and offended...and troubled the Church with your Errors and have drawen away many a poor soule, and have upheld your Revelations; and forasmuch as you have made a Lye...Therefor in the name of our Lord Je[sus] Ch[rist]...I doe cast you out and...deliver you up to Sathan...and account you from this time forth to be a Hethen and a Publican...I command you in the name of Ch[rist] Je[sus] and of this Church as a Leper to withdraw your selfe out of the Congregation.

It's ironic that a minister who left his church in England because of his nonconformist views would find himself in the role of deciding in his adopted land what people could and could not believe as members of the church there. Wilson also tried to convert the Native Americans to Christianity. In the 1650s, Quakers also came to the Massachusetts Bay Colony, where they were not tolerated by the new ministers from England. In fact, on October 27, 1659, three Quakers, Marmaduke Stevenson, William Robinson, and Mary Dyer, were led to the Boston gallows from the prison where they had been held for their Quaker "evangelism," and Wilson was there when the two men were executed. Mary Dyer, a former member of his church, received a last-minute reprieve. She ended up on the gallows a year later, where Wilson called out to her to repent: "Mary Dyer, O repent, O repent, and be not so deluded and carried away by deceit of the devil." Her reply was, "Nay, man, I am not now to repent." Then she was hanged. So much for religious tolerance in the new world.

Another Separatist minister I can claim as my relative is **Francis Johnson**. Born in 1562 in North Riding, Yorkshire, England, he is my great-grandfather ten generations back. In 1592, he was imprisoned for his nonconformist religious beliefs in England along with his brother

George. However, Francis and George were ultimately released from prison and sailed to Amsterdam. There Francis served as a minister to other exiled separatists. But he still would not find peace because while he was in prison in 1594 he had married **Thomasine Boyes**. She was considered a fancy dresser. This was seen as inappropriate by some of his congregants and especially offensive to her brother-in-law George. My great-grandmother's manner of dress was not seen as elegant or fashionable but rather as sexually provocative and prideful. Great-Uncle George apparently wrote many letters about this topic to his brother because he wanted to show Thomasine "that proud apparel and fashions of worldly dames were not decent in a Pastor's wife." She liked to wear velvet, lace, whalebone, and even gold.

This dispute over the proper attire for a minister's wife went on for years until Johnson's father came over from England to try to resolve the issue between the brothers in 1598–9. Francis ultimately excommunicated both his father and brother from the church.

Apparently, just being a Separatist didn't necessarily mean people would be more tolerant of differences in behavior. This is evident in George Johnson's letters and the behavior of other congregants who supported his views about Thomasine's manner of dress. Based on what I have read, I think the Puritans came down hard on people that didn't toe the line in terms of dress, words, or deeds.

I would like to clarify the terminology I am using. Separatists, also known as Pilgrims, didn't want to be part of the Church of England. They were Christian but wanted to worship God in a manner of their choosing in the New World. This initial group of about one hundred people sailing on the *Mayflower* first settled in Plymouth, Massachusetts, in 1620.

Puritans, who came to New England in greater numbers, still wanted to be connected to the Church of England. Indeed, when about one thousand Puritans arrived in Boston in 1630, they had an official charter from the King of England to establish the Massachusetts Bay

Colony. They considered themselves part of the Anglican Church but wanted a purified version of this faith, rather than one similar to what was practiced in England after Henry VIII established his own church there. They thought that version was too similar to the Catholic faith and its traditions, and they didn't want any part of it.

Puritans Could Be Harsh

Once the Puritans came to the colonies, they monitored the behavior of other settlers so that any "freedom" some people might have sought when they left England wasn't always at hand. Within ten years of their arrival, Puritans had settled in Massachusetts, Connecticut, and parts of Long Island, New York. My great-grandfather ten generations back was Englishman **Thomas Ufford**. He sailed on the ship Lion for the British Colonies on June 22, 1632, accompanied by his wife and three children, including son John, my ancestor, who was six years old at that time. Once in America, this family settled in Milford, Connecticut, by 1644, following Puritan Minister Peter Prudden there.

His son John grew up in New England and married Hannah Hawley in Milford, Connecticut, in 1656. But on March 25, 1657, John Ufford was forced to appear before the court in New Haven, accused of "committing fornication with Martha Nettleton," his father's servant. During this Puritan time in America, people were brought to court for having sex with someone who was not their spouse. Earlier, wife Hannah Hawley had appeared before the same court, accusing John of not being able to perform his "husbandly duty" with her. She was granted a divorce on these grounds. The members of the court were shocked to find that someone who couldn't perform his husbandly duty and had himself admitted in the divorce case that he wasn't fit for that relationship would find himself in this situation. The court order states: "Now it is a strange thing, that after all this he should miscarry in this manner."

Apparently poor great-grandpa John Ufford had sex with Martha and she was pregnant. The court was shocked about this. Looking at this case from the viewpoint of someone living in the twenty-first century with much more relaxed attitudes about who has sex with whom, this seems so funny. But I doubt John thought it was funny. He sounded like he was afraid and remorseful as he confessed to the court that "he had committed filthyness with this woman, Martha Nettleton, and that she was with child by him." Furthermore, John Ufford told the court he was sorry for his sin committed against God.

Once this pregnancy came to light, the court decided they needed to talk to Hannah Hawley again about what she alleged against poor John. Once they did so, the magistrate found that Hannah had been in error in her allegation. No kidding! Poor John, his infidelity with his father's servant will be read about for centuries going forward by both genealogists and historians. But he did the honorable thing and married Martha Nettleton. Their daughter **Mary Ufford** is my great-grandmother eight generations back. I wonder what she thought about what her father had done when she heard about it?

Going from one country to another didn't necessarily mean more freedom to do as one pleases. In some cases, leaving was motivated by other reasons, such as not being able to earn a living because wealthy landowners, with government support, were pushing you off the land your family had lived on for centuries. This is what happened to many of my Scottish ancestors.

Scottish Relatives Flee After Highland Clearances

While growing my family tree, I pay special attention if ancestors from different branches are emigrating from the same country during the same time period. This typically means something is happening in that country forcing people to flee.

My paternal great-grandfathers four generations back left Scotland for Canada in 1815. They were **John MacCrimmon**, a great-grandfather of my great-grandmother **Rosa Cook**, and **William Oliver**, a great-grandfather of my great-grandmother **Christina MacKay**. Duncan MacCrimmon was the great-grandfather of my grandpa Bopa, who I mentioned earlier. His wife Norma Zealand, whose family I also wrote about earlier, was great-great-granddaughter to William Oliver.

So what was happening in 1815 that made these ancestors leave Scotland? This is the year that the Napoleonic Wars ended and many fighting Scottish men returned home. During the war, there had been a twelve-year hiatus of people immigrating from Scotland to Canada or America. When these soldiers returned, they found their land overpopulated and the economy in bad shape. The British government wanted to avoid problems at home after the Napoleonic Wars ended while also wanting to strengthen its border of British colonies in Canada against the Americans after the War of 1812. As a result, on February 22, 1815, the Bathurst Proclamation was enacted: a new policy to encourage and subsidize Scottish people to emigrate to Canada. This is why so many Scottish people left their homeland in 1815. These people were better off than many Scots who had immigrated to Canada earlier because the government helped by providing food, transport, and land grants this time.

The "Highland Clearances" were becoming more commonplace. This was when wealthy landlords pushed Scottish people off their lands toward coastal communities and beyond in order to raise sheep on the land. Sheep raising was thought to be more profitable as wool was in demand and the animals could also be slaughtered for mutton. By 1811, an estimated fifteen thousand Scottish tenants had been moved from the land they had lived on for centuries to make way for sheep raising. People who moved to coastal areas were expected to make a living raising kelp. Since there were too many people doing this, it led to a collapse of the kelp industry. People could no longer make a living in Scotland, so many of them left for Canada or America.

My relatives were among them. John MacCrimmon sailed with 122 other passengers, including his wife and siblings, on the ship Eliza on August 3, 1815. They sailed from Greenock, Scotland, to Quebec, Canada. Three other ships called the Atlas, Baltic Merchant, and Dorothy made the same journey over that summer, carrying hundreds of Scottish citizens to Canada. Here is a list of the passengers on the Eliza, including my great-grandfather John MacCrimmon and members of his family. http://www.theshipslist.com/ships/passengerlists/eliza1815.shtml.

This entire group of passengers on the four ships were known as the "Edinburgh Settlers." They arrived at the port of Quebec in early October. More than half of the seven hundred people who came on the four ships settled in Lochiel Township in Glengarry County, Canada, at least at first. Later on, generations spread out among different areas in that part of Canada.

Relative William Oliver also came to Canada from Scotland in 1815 at the age of fifteen. His father John, a farmer, was forty years old. The Oliver family came over on the Baltic Merchant ship during the same summer as great-grandfather John MacCrimmon came over on the Eliza. Here is a link to the ship's list of passengers, including

William Oliver, his father John, mother Mary Munn, and five siblings: http://www.theshipslist.com/ships/passengerlists/balticm1815.shtml.

Most likely, John Oliver made the decision to leave Scotland for the same reason as Duncan MacCrimmon: better economic opportunities in Canada. Even today, people move for the same reason, to have an opportunity to make a living for themselves and their families. When you are growing your tree, make sure to pay attention to certain years or periods of several years that keep showing up among different immigrant relatives, like 1815 in this case. Often times, something is happening in the political or economic situation of a country that is forcing people to flee, such as religious persecution of Protestants in France or religious and political turmoil in England in the 1520s and 1530s.

How Far Back Does Your Tree Go?

One of the fun challenges of genealogy is to see how far back you can get your tree to go and still maintain its legitimacy. Thanks to my royal connection to John the Fearless, my great-grandfather twenty generations ago, my tree goes all the way back to around 400 AD. When you have royals as family, good records are typically kept, and this helps in terms of building one's tree way back into ancient Roman times.

According to Ancestry records, my great-grandfather forty-three generations back is **Tonantius Ferreolus I**, the Praetorian Prefect of Gaul. He is said to have been born in Rome around 400. His biography appears in Wikipedia, where it says he lived from c. 390 to 475. Five generations of Gaul-Romans later, all of whom were based in France, we arrive at great-grandfather **Saint Arnulfe**, my great-grandfather thirty-nine generations ago. He was born August 12, 582, in Liege, Belgium. When he was an adult, he became bishop of Metz in Belgium. His sister was called **Saint Itta Idoberg of Nivelles**. Saint Itta, my great-grandmother thirty-eight generations back, made a name for herself by marrying **Pepin I**, Mayor of the Palace of Austrasia. Austrasia includes present day northeastern France and western and central Germany, with Metz as its capital.

This couple sired **Saint Begga of Landen**. Their son was Pepin II, himself the Mayor of Austrasia after his grandfather of the same name. Pepin II and an unnamed concubine gave birth to **Charles "The Hammer" Martel**, who subsequently became the mayor of Austrasia.

Charles Martel's wife gave birth to another Pepin! He was **Pepin III Martel**. He was called Pepin the Short because he wasn't a big guy. Nonetheless, he and his wife **Bertha of Leon** were the parents of **Charlemagne**, born in 742 in Germany.

Everyone has heard of Charlemagne, and many Europeans are related to him. He is my great-grandfather thirty-three generations back. In fact, a fun genealogical fact is that everyone alive in Europe in the tenth century who left descendants is the ancestor of every living European today, and Charlemagne was an ancestor of some of those tenth-century families. So if your family immigrated from Europe to America, for example, you are probably related to Charlemagne too. Indeed, according to Adam Rutherford, who wrote the book *A Brief History of Everyone Who Ever Lived*, we are all cousins of some degree. He's right. That's what I realized when building my tree.

So Charlemagne, who lived from 742 to 813, was the great king of the Holy Roman Empire. His son, also named Pepin, was King of Italy. He also had a son named **Louis I** (not Pepin!), who had a son named **Louis II**, who himself became the Holy Roman Emperor. These two brothers, with the help of their wives, sired many children who became kings and queens of Europe down through the ages. For instance, the grandson of Louis I was called Louis II and was King of France. He was also called "the Stammerer." I guess he had some kind of speech impediment.

Four generations after Charlemagne's son Pepin lived, his great-great-grandson was born on August 15, 866, in France. He was **Robert I Capet**, who became King of Western France. From his son **Hugh Capet** descended more than a dozen more kings of France, all part of the *Direct Capetians*. His son was also called Hugh. Then thirteen more kings descended directly from the Capets. The Capet Dynasty ended with King Charles IV, who died in 1328 without leaving a male heir. Thus ended a clear line of succession, and ultimately this led to the Hundred Years' War between France and England. King Charles IV's little sister, Isabella Plantagenet, married Edward II, King of England. She was also known as a "she wolf." Just a little hostility toward a strong woman, apparently. Isabella and Edward II were my great-grandparents eighteen generations ago.

Plantagenets are all over my tree, with Isabella giving birth to **King Edward III Plantagenet**. Her grandson was **John Gaunt Plantagenet**.

One of his three wives was **Katherine Roet**, whose sister Philippa was married to Geoffrey Chaucer. So John Gaunt and Chaucer were brothers-in-law. Apparently, they had been close friends before they married the Roet sisters.

One of the children John Gaunt had with his mistress (who later became his third wife) was **John Beaufort**, the first Earl of Somerset. His daughter **Joan Beaufort**, who lived from 1402 to 1445, married well, snagging James Stewart I, King of Scotland. That is when my tree became so Scottish.

Beaufort's second husband, **Sir James Stewart**, was the first earl of Atholl, Scotland, and my great-grandfather fourteen generations back, as noted earlier. They had a son named John Stewart who was born in Scotland in 1440 and died there in 1512. He married **Eleanor Sinclair,** whose father was **William I Sinclair**, Baron of Roslin Castle, in Roslin, Scotland. Together, they had a son also named John, second Earl of Atholl. **Sir John Stewart** had a daughter named **Elizabeth Stewart** around 1513.

She is the reason the Stewart line joined the MacKenzie clan because she married Kenneth MacKenzie in 1538 in Cromarty, Scotland. This MacKenzie came from a long line of MacKenzies as he was the tenth Baron of Kintail, Scotland. Four more generations were MacKenzies. Then my great-grandmother only seven generations back, **Isabella MacKenzie of Seaforth**, married a MacLeod, another big clan name in Scotland, around 1694. Her husband was **Roderick MacLeod**, nineteenth Chief of Clan McLeod.

The next four generations were all MacLeods, including my great-grandfather four generations ago. His name was **Alexander MacLeod**, a sea captain who decided to leave Scotland and immigrate to Canada. On October 18, 1793, they arrived on what is now Prince Edward Island after eighteen weeks at sea. This was their third attempt to leave Scotland by sea voyage.

My DNA results match up with Alexander MacLeod thanks to the existence of several other relatives who took the DNA test and shared their public tree on Ancestry. This is a great way to scientifically verify that your tree is correct, as I noted earlier.

Besides MacKenzie and MacLeod ancestors, I have many MacCrimmon relations. This is a clan famous for piping throughout the generations, with a special relationship as pipers for the MacLeod family. I will talk more about this shortly.

My great-great-grandmother was **Mary McCrimmon**. As a twenty-one-year-old man, her father, **Duncan MacCrimmon**, immigrated from Scotland to Canada in 1815. He sailed with 122 other passengers, including his parents, on the ship *Eliza,* with Captain Telfer at the helm. They sailed from Greenock, Scotland, to Quebec, Canada, along with three other ships, the *Atlas*, the *Baltic Merchant*, and the *Dorothy*.

As noted in the last chapter, the Bathurst Proclamation was signed into law February 22, 1815. This proclamation established a policy to encourage and help subsidize Scottish people to emigrate to Canada. Many Scottish citizens left for Canada after this policy was enacted, such as great-grandfather Duncan MacCrimmon. These "Edinburgh Settlers" were transported to Canada by the government and given land when they arrived. One of three locations these immigrants were taken to from Quebec, up the St. Lawrence River to Upper Canada, was Lochiel Township in Glengarry County. As I noted earlier, more than half of the seven hundred people who participated in this program settled in northern Glengarry.

Duncan's wife, **Mary MacLeod**, came to Canada as an infant with her family, including father Alexander MacLeod, in 1793. Five years after Duncan MacCrimmon arrived in Glengarry County, he married Mary MacLeod. As I mentioned, the MacCrimmons and MacLeods had a special relationship going back centuries, so it's not surprising these two clans hooked up via my great-grandparents' marriage.

My great-grandfather seven generations back was **Padruig Og MacCrimmon**. He was a very well-known musician from Borreraig, on the Isle of Skye, in Scotland. He also operated a music school there where he taught other people to play the bagpipes. In the book *The MacCrimmons of Skye, Hereditary Pipers to the MacLeods of Dunvegan*, author Fred T. MacLeod writes about the special relationship between these two families.

In 1625, **Rory Mor MacLeod**, a much-loved leader of his clan living in Dunvegan Castle, passed away. He was my great-grandfather nine generations ago and the fifteenth chief of Clan MacLeod. Apparently this clan leader was a most special man. According to Fred MacLeod's book, Rory was "warrior and statesman, patron of music, art and of letters and dispenser of lavish hospitality to rich and poor alike." Upon Rory MacLeod's death, Padraig MacCrimmon went from Dunvegan Castle to his College of Pipers in Borreraig to play the bagpipes for his pupils in honor of his great patron. There, with great emotion, he played a piece of music called "Lament to Rory Mor," according to Fred MacLeod's interesting book about the relationship between the two well-known Scottish clans. Padraig MacCrimmon composed the largest number of pipe tunes among this family. "Lament for the Children," a well-known piece of music he wrote and played, expressed his profound sadness over the death of six of his seven sons, reportedly from smallpox. Only one son survived. He composed a piece for this son titled "The Lament for the Only Son."

The surviving son was **Padruig Og MacCrimmon**, my great-grandfather seven generations back. According to public family trees, he lived from around 1645 to 1730. Like his father and namesake, son Padraig was a piper who entertained the MacLeods of Dunvegan Castle. He also trained many other pipers at his music school in Borreraig. According to Fred MacLeod's book, this Padruig wasn't as well-known as his father and was more of a music teacher than an original composer. He and his wife did have twenty children, however, and that's quite an accomplishment in my book.

One of his sons was **Malcolm MacLeod**, 1695–1769, who continued the piping family tradition. He was also my great-grandfather six generations back. One of his children, **Iain Dubh MacCrimmon**, also my great-grandfather, was the last MacCrimmon to continue the piping tradition. He resided in Scotland from 1730 to 1822, living to be over ninety years old according to Fred MacLeod's book. He thought about migrating to America, as many other Scottish people were starting to do at the end of the 1700s and in the early 1800s. He got as far as Greenock, Scotland, and then changed his mind and went back home. He is buried in Kilmuir Churchyard, in Dunvegan.

He was an interesting character too. According to the book *History of the Clan MacCrimmon*, by George C. B. Poulter,

> Iain Dubh and his family are said by Simon Fraser to have been religious folk with broad and advanced views which brought them into conflict with the local ministers, who at that time were often narrow-minded and intolerant. Iain and his predecessors had composed verses for some of their piobaireachds (pipe players) and these are also alleged to have aroused the anger of the local ministers. Shortly before his death, Iain Dubh wrote a pamphlet on "The Failure of Christianity," which, according to Simon Fraser, so annoyed the clergy that they had a copy of it buried with him in his grave.

Sounds like a man I would have liked. One of his many children, **John MacCrimmon**, my great-grandfather four generations ago, decided that given many relatives were leaving Scotland, the time was right for him to emigrate. He arrived in Ontario, Canada, on August 3, 1815, on the ship Eliza, which I mentioned earlier. He was one of the Edinburgh settlers, Scottish people coming to Canada with the promise of land from the English government.

A Deep Dive Into One Tree Branch: The Adams Family from Ireland

After you have grown your tree back as far as possible with verification of facts by some public records, it can also be interesting to look at what recent relatives have accomplished. Through doing genealogical searches, you can find this out. For example, I discovered that the younger sister of my great-grandmother from Ireland, Rosa Mary Adams, had a sister named **Catherine Ashmore Adams** who had a most interesting life. She met and married a Japanese man named **Sonzo Tamagawa**. They both worked as silk merchants for Corticelli Silk Company in Yokohama, Japan, helping to export silk from Japan to buyers elsewhere, including in America. Catherine and her husband were in Yokohama when a 7.9 magnitude earthquake hit this city on September 1, 1923.

Catherine Adams had a daughter named **Kathleen Adams Tamagawa**. She authored a book about her experience as a half-Japanese, half-Northern-Irish woman titled *Holy Prayers in a Horse's Ear*. My first cousin two generations removed wrote about how she didn't feel like she belonged in either culture. The time period in which my cousin lived in Japan was from 1907, when she was thirteen, until she got married to an American at nineteen years old and then moved to the US in 1915, when she was twenty-one years old.

In her book, my cousin also included letters from her mother describing what she saw and did during the terrible earthquake of 1923. I found this part of the book of great interest. My great-grandaunt Catherine, in a letter to a friend, described what happened when the earthquake hit, at noon on September 1, 1923. She got up from her chair after her maid announced it was time for tiffin (a light midday meal) and the house bounced up, like an explosion had happened underneath it. She was thrown across the room and the house came down on top of her! Then she heard the "cracking of fire" and thought that this was how she and two maids in the house with her would die. She had broken bones and was bleeding from a cut on her head. Despite her pain, she wiggled her way out of the rubble. She staggered across her lawn and ended up clinging to a tree. From this vantage point, she looked around and noticed that not one house was left standing. She likened the experience to "Judgment Day." She then searched for people to help her rescue the two maids even with fires all around. She found some teenage boys and together they battered a hole in the roof of her house. One of the smaller boys went through the hole despite the smoke and heat all round them. Luckily, he was able to rescue both maids, one who had almost lost her ear and the other who had a broken arm.

This earthquake devastated Tokyo, Yokohama, and other cities in the region. Fires started shortly after the quake, some of which turned into firestorms. The water mains also broke, making it harder to put out the fires. An estimated 142,800 people died from the earthquake and its terrible aftermath.

The eighth day after the catastrophic earthquake, her husband arrived, "ragged, dirty and lame." Unfortunately, he then decided to walk from their house to Kobe, in the hopes of cabling from there to his firm. Since this involved a walk of fifty miles through a devastated area, she didn't go with him. After he left, Catherine never saw her Japanese husband again because she left Japan and moved to New York that same year to be with her daughter and son-in-law. According to Holy Prayers in a Horse's Ear, Catherine worried that she might get pneumonia if she went back to Japan to be with her husband, as she had gotten it once before in Japan. Ironically, my great-grandaunt died six years later of pneumonia, which she had acquired in New Rochelle, New York.

Catherine Adams came from a family of risk-takers. Her father, **Richard Adams**, my second great-grandfather, was the son of the wool merchant Francis Adams, who I wrote about earlier. Francis gave money to his son as a wedding gift after he was married in Dublin to **Elizabeth Frances Murrow** in 1852. Richard then used this money to sail with his wife to Australia in search of gold! So that's where my great-granduncle Francis and my great-grandmother Rosa Mary Adams were born. While doing my genealogical work, I was able to obtain birth certificates for both Francis and Rosa from the Australian government. They were both born in Geelong, Australia. I uploaded these documents to my tree on Ancestry to document their births and to give others a chance to put this information in their trees as well.

The risky step of sailing to Australia with his new wife in search of gold didn't work out, perhaps because he wasn't able to find any gold himself. So a few years later, they returned to Northern Ireland and had Catherine Adams in Londonderry. But they didn't stay there long either, deciding to emigrate to the United States. The Adams family arrived in New York on April 14, 1885, the day President Abraham Lincoln was shot.

Richard Adams's brother, **George Forbes Adams**, led an interesting life as well. He studied at Trinity College in Dublin and became a doctor. He traveled widely around the world, according to public records of his arrival and departure, to places like Hong Kong, New Zealand, and New Caledonia in the South Pacific. George Adams served with Major General Charles Gordon of Khartoum, a British army officer and administrator, after he participated in the Crimean War from 1853 to 1856. My great-granduncle two generations back was a staff assistant surgeon for the British Army in Hong Kong from 1863 to 1870.

Another brother of Richard Adams was **Alfred Adams**. He also attended Trinity College in Dublin, just like his brother George and my great-grandfather Richard. Later he got married at the British Embassy in Paris. He must not have been happy in that life as he then signed up to be a soldier in Garibaldi's Army. Giuseppe Garibaldi fought to unite northern and southern Italy, using a volunteer army of guerrilla soldiers, including my great-uncle Alfred. After the conflict ended in 1861, Alfred didn't return home. He died on January 21, 1876, in Frankfurt, Germany, at only thirty-seven years old. I found his death certificate in German on Ancestry and uploaded it to Alfred's page on my family tree, *Blodgetts and Delands through the Ages.*

The Adams sons were an adventuresome, well-traveled group of men. Their two sisters, Mary Anne Ashmore Adams and Catherine Hope Adams, were also well-traveled. Indeed, they spent much of their lives in Florence, Italy. It was Catherine Hope Adams whose grave I unsuccessfully tried to track down when I was in Florence a few years ago. Wool merchant Francis Adams had six sons altogether, three with his first wife, who later died, and three with his second wife, my great-grandmother *Isabella Rankin.* One of the sons of his first wife was William R. Adams. And wouldn't you know it? He also went to Trinity College in Dublin, graduating in 1836. Later on, he decided to leave his family in Ireland as well, moving to the United States in 1839. Once there, he attended and graduated from the General Theological Seminary of the Episcopal Church in 1841. He then moved to Wisconsin and helped start Nashotah House, an Anglican seminary in Nashotah, Wisconsin, in 1842. This seminary school is still in operation today. In fact, its campus was listed on the National Register of Historic Places in 2017. Because of his role in setting up this seminary and his role as educator at Nashotah House, his biography is on Wikipedia. Rev. William Adams also published articles in several periodicals, writing primarily on theological topics. https://en.wikipedia.org/wiki/William_Adams_(educator).

The Wikipedia entry for my great-granduncle two generations ago also includes a portrait of him. Since this work of art is now in the public domain, I include it here.

Rev. William Adams

Rev. William Adams married **Elizabeth Marius Kemper** in 1848. She was the daughter of Bishop **Jackson Kemper**, a published author and well-known religious figure. In 1835, he became the first missionary bishop of the Episcopal Church in the US. He has a more extensive biography in Wikipedia as well as many other places: https://en.wikipedia.org/wiki/Jackson_Kemper.

He reportedly ordained William Adams and helped him with setting up Nashotah House. He also presided over the marriage of William Adams and his own daughter Elizabeth. In the Episcopal/ Anglican Church, he is noteworthy. For example, Kemper is honored with a feast day on the liturgical calendar of the Episcopal Church and the Anglican Church in North America on May 24.

In 1870, when Rev. Williams was fifty-seven years old, he appeared in the US Census records with his wife Elizabeth and other family members. Although the year of his birth was correctly stated as 1813, the report about this record said his profession was "Prof Shoe Serving." However, if you look at the image of the census record rather than at the written record, it clearly states that he is a professor of a theological seminary. I point this out so that you make sure to look at the images if available when doing genealogical work, rather than assume that the public record is correct. On May 11, 2021, an Ancestry member reported this transcription error. However, as of this date in 2023, no correction has been made to this mistake in US Census records. It just goes to show you what I said in the first part of this book. That is, don't trust such public records to always get everything right!

The granddaughter of William and Elizabeth Adams, **Elizabeth Kemper Adams**, was also a person of note. My second cousin two generations removed, she was born in Nashotah, Wisconsin, in 1872 to **Francis Kemper Adams** and **Mary Lee Whiting**. She graduated from Vassar College in 1893 and went on to get a PhD at the University of Chicago in 1904, well before many women earned advanced degrees. Her dissertation was titled "The Aesthetic Experience: Its Meaning in a Functional Psychology." The next year, she became a philosophy professor at Smith College. In 1911, she became the first director of the school's education department. She retired from Smith College in 1916, and in the 1920s she became the national education secretary for the Girl Scouts of the USA. Her biography is also on Wikipedia, where it states that she was an American psychologist and historian of education. She also published many articles and published a poem in The Atlantic magazine. https://en.wikipedia.org/wiki/Elizabeth_Kemper_Adams.

This is just one branch of my family on my mother's side and look at how many interesting stories I was able to uncover. Perhaps you can do the same if you take a deep dive into your family tree?

Keeping Your Tree Alive After You Are Gone

After all the work you have done to grow a top-notch family tree, it's important to think about who will tend to this project when you are gone. My understanding is that once you build a tree on Ancestry, it won't go away unless it is deleted by its owner or by someone who has been granted rights to be an editor of the account. Another option is to create a tree with MyHeritage. This is a good family tree site as well, but there is a fee to subscribe.

One thing I have done to help keep family members involved in the family tree is to invite them by email to be a contributor to my tree. This way, they can also upload documents or factual information to the tree and feel involved. They don't have to pay for a subscription to be a contributor to your account. However, if towards the end of your life you decide to give up your editorship of the account, you will want to find someone else in the family willing to take it over and pay the monthly fee for the account. As of the time of this writing, the subscription fee was forty-three dollars a month for an Ancestry account that gives access to records worldwide.

Since I am working on my tree at least once a week, if not more, that amount of money is well worth the cost. Genealogy is my main hobby. It's a great pastime for people with lots of free time, such as retired folks like me.

If you have taken time to grow a family tree on FamilySearch, people can access your tree for free, making it easier to encourage a family member to work on the tree from time to time without cost. Your tree there can also be modified by members of the general public. This can be a good thing if you want others to help you build your family tree or correct any mistakes that may exist. But if you want to have complete control of who and what is on your tree, this is impossible on FamilySearch.

Conclusion

Growing my family tree helped me appreciate who I am and what "good stock" I come from, as my mother used to say to me, and her mother used to say to her. I had no idea how Scottish I was until I took the Ancestry DNA test and kept building my tree further and further back. As I said at the beginning of this book, researching one's ancestors really helps you go deeper in understanding your heritage.

Hopefully, reading this book will help you not only grow a great tree but will help you realize how many family stories await your discovery when you take time to pursue genealogy.

I consider building a family tree to be sacred work, as it is a way to honor your ancestors and learn more about who you truly are. When I am working on my tree, I am sending a message out into the universe that my parents, grandparents, and great-grandparents through the ages matter to me and that their heritage matters to me. It is holy work.

List of Ancestors Mentioned

Adams, Alfred
    Adams, Catherine Ashmore
    Adams, Catherine Hope Adams
    Elizabeth Kemper Adams
    Francis Adams
    Francis Kemper Adams
    George Forbes Adams
    Mary Ann Ashmore Adams
    Rosa Mary Adams
    William Alfonso VIII of Castille Aquitaine
    Eleanor of Arnulfe
    Saint Bacon
    Francis Beauclerc
    Henry I Beauclerk
    Matilda Beaufort
    Joan Beaufort
    John Bethune
    John Ferquhard Birdsey
    Abel Birdsey
    Jonas Abel Birdsey
    Phebe Blodgett
    Charles Warren Blodgett
    Cyrus Blodgett
    Archippus Blodgett
    Fred Blodgett
    Henry Blodgett
    Samuel Blodgett
    Thomas Blodgett
    Virginia Blodgett
    Warren William Blodgett

Bibliography

Haxtun, Annie Armoux. (1896) *Signers of the Mayflower Compact.* Baltimore, Maryland. Genealogical Publishing Company.

Hotten, John Camden. (1874) *The Original Lists of Persons of Quality, 1600-1700.* London, England. Reprinted in 2003 by Genealogical Publishing Company.

Johnson, Caleb. (2007) *Here Shall I Die Ashore.* Bloomington, Indiana. Xlibris publisher.

Leach Rixford, E. (1932) *Families Directly Descended from All Royal Families in Europe* (495 to 1932) and Mayflower Descendants. Burlington, Vermont. Free Press Printing.

Lewis Weis, F. (2004) *Ancestral Roots of Certain American Colonists Who Came to America Before 1700, Eighth Edition.* Baltimore, Maryland. Genealogical Publishing Company.

MacKenzie, A. (1889) *History of the MacLeods With Genealogies of the Principal Families of the Name.* Inverness, Scotland. A & W MacKenzie.

MacLeod, Fred. T. (1933) *The MacCrimmons of Skye: Hereditary Pipers to the MacLeods of Dunvegan.* Edinburgh, Scotland. Henderson & Henderson.

MacLeod, Rev. Cannon R.C. (1927) *The MacLeods of Dunvegan.* Edinburgh, Scotland. Henderson & Hamilton.

Massie, Allan. (2010) *The Royal Stuarts.* London, England. Random House.

Poulter, George, C.B. (1991) *History of the Clan MacCrimmon.* Camberley, England: Clan MacCrimmon Society.

Roach, Marilynne. (2004) *The Salem Witch Trials: A Day-by-Day Chronicle of a Community Under Siege.* Boulder, Colorado. Taylor Trade Publishing.

Tamagawa, Kathleen. (1932) *Holy Prayers in a Horse's Ear.* New York. Ray Long & Richard R. Smith, Inc.

Acknowledgments

Special recognition goes to my friend Darlene Foster, a fellow published author of many books, including the Amanda Travels book series for children and her most recent book, *You Can Take the Girl from the Prairie: Stories about Growing Up on the Canadian Prairies.*

Darlene helped me edit all my books and has encouraged and advised me regarding marketing. For more information about Darlene, check out her blog, https://darlenefoster.wordpress.com.

I also want to thank the members of the Torrevieja Writers' Circle who encouraged me to write this book about genealogy after hearing me read the story about my Zealand ancestors entitled "Six Generations of Sad Endings." That story is included in this book.

Finally, I want to thank editor and author Molly Ringle for doing a final edit of my book to make sure its style conformed to *The Chicago Manual of Style*, with particular attention to capitalization, formatting, punctuation and numbers.

About the Author

This is Nancy Blodgett Klein's fourth book. Her other books are:

Torn Between Worlds: A Mexican Immigrant's Journey to Find Herself (2021)

Isabel, a twelve-year-old Mexican girl, struggles as she tries to settle into a new life in the United States. She misses her mother, left behind when she and her father came to find a better life. She doesn't feel welcome living with her uncle and his family and struggles with the English language. How will she cope in this strange new world?

Her kind sixth-grade teacher suggests Isabel keep a journal, where she can pour out the feelings she used to share with her mother. She encourages her to take home the newspaper to help improve her English and learn about world events. While Isabel starts to make friends, she is horrified by the events that take place on September 11, 2001, in the US, witnesses a deadly political demonstration in Oaxaca, Mexico, and is eventually forced to flee to Madrid, Spain.

Will all this chaos prevent Isabel from finding a way to feel connected to the world around her? This coming-of-age story is written in journal format, spanning three years and three countries. Follow Isabel as she grows into a young woman during turbulent times, trying to find a place to call home instead of feeling torn between worlds.

Life Lessons: Guidance for All Ages (2021)

This is an anthology of thirty-four stories from a variety of authors sharing experiences that happened to them and concluding with what each author learned as a result. Each touching story begins with a quote related to the subject, shares the experience, and concludes with a moral. This collection of stories is especially geared towards younger people who may need some guidance about how to successfully navigate their lives. However, people of all ages would find this book of interest because of the variety of wonderful stories and moral guidance shared. Some stories are happy while others are quite sad. In all cases, these mature writers share lessons from their own experiences to help others successfully navigate through the ups and downs of life.

What's So Special about Spain? (2022)

This is a book meant for children to help them understand what makes Spain so special by highlighting some of its more interesting cities through words and plenty of color photos. Adults can use the book to help them plan a trip to Spain as well. The tour of Spain is designed so that visitors to the country can travel via car or public transportation in a clockwise direction to see the most important sights in nine unique cities of the country. Generally, the cities are between three to five hours apart. Most of these places have been designated as World Heritage Sites by UNESCO.

Praise for the Author

Torn Between Worlds tells the story of a Mexican girl who leaves her homeland to live in the United States and Spain. Told in journal entries, the girl's story pivots around the economic and political realities that necessitate her moves. She must adapt to different lifestyles and languages as she grows into young womanhood. Her strength and insightfulness make her a heroine girls can look up to.

Amazon.co.uk review

Superb account of growing up from the diary of a young Mexican girl, who at the age of twelve finds herself in the United States with her father but separated from her mother. She not only has to learn a new language but to fit into a new way of life. The story encompasses three years and three continents and includes the terrorist attack of 9/11 in America at the beginning and the terror attack of the Madrid train bombing at the end. Contains more sadness than joy, and yet one is left with a wonderful sense of achievement for the narrator. A must for pre-teenage girls, but also a great read for adults. You won't put it down until the end.

Amazon.ca review

I love reading stories written in journal format as you really get to know the main character. Young people especially are very honest about their feelings and thoughts when writing in their journal. The author has done a great job writing from the point of view of a young immigrant girl sharing her innermost thoughts as she deals with trying to fit in, a new language and frightening current events. Isabel is living in the United States at the time of the 9/11 attacks. A scary time for all young people but even more so for immigrant children. She documents her fears, joys, ideas and hopes as she moves between Mexico, the US, and Spain. We learn about her friends, her first kiss and how she deals with her parents' failing marriage. Growing up is never easy, but for Isabel, it's especially difficult. I highly recommend this book.

Amazon.es reviews

Torn Between Worlds gripped me from the start: Isabel keeps a journal of her life in three different countries, and we see how world events impact her development as she recounts her questions, fears and dreams. It is written with such innocent clarity it's hard to believe an adult wrote it: the author certainly creates her character's world so personally that we feel we really know young Isabel.

It follows the story of a Mexican girl, Isabel Martinez-Estrada. She illegally enters the US with her father when only nine years old. Once in Chicago, she tells you about her everyday life and the kind teacher who understands what she is going through and helps her along the way. You hear about her family and friends, and the devastating impact the terrorist attack on 9/11 brings to her and her friends.

After three years of missing her home and her mother and grandparents she and her father head back to Mexico. In Mexico, she finds her mother doing dangerous work demonstrating to help teachers have better pay. While there, she finds herself torn between the USA and the life she lived before. She feels like a person without a country to call her own.

Reviews of *Life Lessons*

Amazon.com

Right from the first page this book had grabbed me. I think the concept is great, and it was interesting reading all the different authors, and seeing their different walks of life, and how those life experiences shaped them. Overall, the book was entertaining and powerful! I highly recommend it!

Amazon.co.uk

Well written book of short tales of how we learn from everyday happenings. Age makes most people wiser, lots of lovely little life learnings. Some funny some sad and some just life!

Reviews of *What's So Special about Spain?*

Amazon.ca

A wonderful book describing some of the many wonders of Spain with amazing pictures and interesting details. Children and their parents will enjoy planning a future trip with ideas from this book, or just learning about special places and things to do in Spain.

Amazon.co.uk

A well written children's book about Spain. My grandchildren enjoyed reading about Spanish areas. They can't wait to do some of the trips.

Don't miss out!

Visit the website below and you can sign up to receive emails whenever Nancy Blodgett Klein publishes a new book. There's no charge and no obligation.

https://books2read.com/r/B-A-PMZDB-UIMDD

BOOKS2READ

Connecting independent readers to independent writers.

Did you love *Growing a Top-Notch Family Tree with Stories from its Branches*? Then you should read *Life Lessons: Guidance for All Ages*[1] by Nancy Blodgett Klein!

This is an anthology of 34 true stories from a variety of authors sharing their experiences and concluding with what they learned as a result. Each touching story begins with a quote related to the subject, shares the experience or events, and concludes with a moral. This collection of stories is geared towards younger people who may need some guidance about how to successfully navigate their lives. However, people of all ages would find this book of interest because of the variety of wonrderful stories and moral guidance shared. Some stories are happy while others are quite sad. In all cases, these mature writers share lessons

---

1. https://books2read.com/u/4XY5n6

2. https://books2read.com/u/4XY5n6

from their own experiences to help others naviage through the ups and downs of life.

Read more at https://www.spainwriter.home.blog.

Also by Nancy Blodgett Klein

Life Lessons: Guidance for All Ages
Torn Between Worlds
What's So Special About Spain?
Growing a Top-Notch Family Tree with Stories from its Branches
Poetry for Troubled Times

Watch for more at https://www.spainwriter.home.blog.

About the Author

Nancy Blodgett Klein worked as a journalist as well as a magazine editor in the Chicagoland area for much of her career after receiving a master's degree in journalism from Boston University. Later on, she went back to college and earned as master's degree from Roosevelt University in Illinois. Then she worked as a bilingual teacher to mostly Mexican students. In 2016, she retired to Spain with her husband Rick Klein. They are the proud parents of two adult sons named Alex and Andy.

While living in Spain, Nancy keeps busy with yoga, singing in a choir, participating in a writers group and two book groups. She also writes a blog on a variety of topics called spainwriter.home.blog.

Nancy Blodgett Klein worked as a journalist as well as a magazine editor in the Chicagoland area for much of her career after receiving a master's degree in journalism from Boston University. Later on, she went back to college and earned as master's degree from Roosevelt University in Illinois. Then she worked as a bilingual teacher to mostly

Mexican students. In 2016, she retired to Spain with her husband Rick Klein. They are the proud parents of two adult sons named Alex and Andy.

While living in Spain, Nancy keeps busy with yoga, singing in a choir, participating in a writers group and two book groups. She also writes a blog on a variety of topics called spainwriter.home.blog.

Read more at https://www.spainwriter.home.blog.